出境领队英语

主　编　朱　华
副主编　闻　华　王雪霏

内容简介

本书是在新修订的《中华人民共和国旅游法》的基础上,为满足大专院校教学、旅游企业培训、导游转型成为出境领队编写而成。本书采用"互联网+"教材的编写理念,融视、听、说、读、写、译为一体,通过扫描二维码,即可获取出境领队英语的视、听、说、读、写、译等教学资源。本书以出境领队带团为主线,按领队业务操作流程编写教学内容,涵盖领队服务全过程,包括"出团前的准备""中国出境""飞行途中""抵达目的地""联系地陪""下榻酒店""观光娱乐""购物与自由活动""安全与应急处理""离境回国"等内容。通过听说、写译、模拟、视频解读、案例分析、角色扮演等,学生可以实现领队英语能力和领队专业能力双融通、双提升。为了方便教学,除了二维码中的教学资源外,本书还为任课教师提供教案和电子课件等。

图书在版编目(CIP)数据

出境领队英语 / 朱华主编. —北京:北京大学出版社,2019.8
(高等院校旅游专业"互联网+"创新规划教材)
ISBN 978-7-301-29434-5

Ⅰ.①出… Ⅱ.①朱… Ⅲ.①旅游—英语—高等学校—教材 Ⅳ.①F59

中国版本图书馆CIP数据核字(2018)第061061号

书　　　名	出境领队英语 CHUJING LINGDUI YINGYU
著作责任者	朱　华　主　编
策划编辑	刘国明
责任编辑	翟　源
数字编辑	陈颖颖
标准书号	ISBN 978-7-301-29434-5
出 版 者	北京大学出版社
地　　　址	北京市海淀区成府路205号　100871
网　　　址	http://www.pup.cn　新浪微博:@北京大学出版社
电子邮箱	编辑部 pup6@pup.cn　总编室 zpup@pup.cn
电　　　话	邮购部 010-62752015　发行部 010-62750672　编辑部 010-62750667
印 刷 者	北京圣夫亚美印刷有限公司
发 行 者	北京大学出版社
经 销 者	新华书店
	787毫米×1092毫米　16开本　9.25印张　210千字 2019年8月第1版　2024年7月第5次印刷
定　　　价	39.00元

未经许可,不得以任何方式复制或抄袭本书之部分或全部内容。
版权所有,侵权必究
举报电话:010-62752024　电子邮箱:fd@pup.cn
图书如有印装质量问题,请与出版部联系,电话:010-62756370

前　言

《中华人民共和国旅游法》第三十九条规定："从事领队业务，应当取得导游证，具有相应的学历、语言能力和旅游从业经历，并与委派其从事领队业务的取得出境旅游业务经营许可的旅行社订立劳动合同。"相关细则解释为：大专以上学历，有外语导游证，或通过大学英语四级以上考试，两年旅游从业经验，并与具有出境旅游业务的旅行社签订合同者，均可以领队身份带团出游。

本书为"互联网+"新型教材，读者通过扫描二维码，即可获取视、听、说、读、写、译等教学资源。本书在编写理念上秉承TAFE教育理念，将技术教育与继续教育、学历教育与职业教育、英语工具性知识和领队专业知识相融通，力争突破传统专业英语教材语言与专业知识割裂分离的"二元结构"，减少导游入职后企业为员工获得领队资格，或提升领队业务能力进行二次培训的成本。

出境领队的服务内容与地陪导游不同，对一个合格的领队的外语能力、工作经验的要求显然比地陪导游、全陪导游高出许多。为此，本书以领队带团为主线，按出境领队业务操作流程编写，涵盖了旅游服务全过程，包括"出团前的准备""中国出境""飞行途中""抵达目的地""联系地陪""下榻酒店""观光娱乐""购物与自由活动""安全与应急处理""离境回国"等教学内容。本书融视、听、说、读、写、译为一体，通过听说、写译、模拟、视频解读、案例分析、角色扮演等再现领队操作流程，努力实现领队英语与领队业务能力培养"二合一"的教学目标。本书由四川师范大学外国语学院教授朱华主编，参加教材编写的还有：闻华、王雪霏、龚晨枫、吕梦莎、韦娟娟、何雯静、吴佳仪。

本书融合了领队教学和培训的主要内容，通过系统学习，读者可实现学历教育和职业教育双融通，增强领队专门用途英语和领队专业知识的应用能力。需要教案、电子课件等教学资源包的老师，可发电子邮件至ernestzhu@126.com索取。

 资源索引　全书 共218个 二维码
◎听力　◎译文　◎视频　◎答案

朱　华
2019年6月25日

目录 Contents

Chapter 1 出团前的准备 1
Preparations Before Departure

Part One Case Study
第一部分：案例分析 2
Part Two Listening Comprehension
第二部分：听力训练 4
Part Three Situational Dialogue
第三部分：情景对话 5
Part Four ABC about Destination Countries
第四部分：目的地国家概况 9
Part Five Consolidation
第五部分：巩固练习 11

Chapter 2 中国出境 15
Departure from China

Part One Case Study
第一部分：案例分析 16
Part Two Listening Comprehension
第二部分：听力训练 18
Part Three Situational Dialogue
第三部分：情景对话 19
Part Four ABC about Destination Countries
第四部分：目的地国家概况 24
Part Five Consolidation
第五部分：巩固练习 26

Chapter 3 飞行途中 29
On the Flight

Part One Case Study
第一部分：案例分析 30
Part Two Listening Comprehension
第二部分：听力训练 31

Part Three Situational Dialogue
第三部分：情景对话..33
Part Four ABC about Destination Countries
第四部分：目的地国家概况..40
Part Five Consolidation
第五部分：巩固练习..43

Chapter 4 抵达目的地 ■45
Arrival at Destination Countries

Part One Case Study
第一部分：案例分析..46
Part Two Listening Comprehension
第二部分：听力训练..47
Part Three Situational Dialogue
第三部分：情景对话..49
Part Four ABC about Destination Countries
第四部分：目的地国家概况..52
Part Five Consolidation
第五部分：巩固练习..54

Chapter 5 联系地陪 ■59
Contact with Local Guides

Part One Case Study
第一部分：案例分析..60
Part Two Listening Comprehension
第二部分：听力训练..61
Part Three Situational Dialogue
第三部分：情景对话..63
Part Four ABC about Destination Countries
第四部分：目的地国家概况..68
Part Five Consolidation
第五部分：巩固练习..70

Chapter 6 下榻酒店 ■73
Hotel Check-in

Part One Case Study
第一部分：案例分析..74
Part Two Listening Comprehension
第二部分：听力训练..75
Part Three Situational Dialogue
第三部分：情景对话..77

Part Four ABC about Destination Countries
第四部分：目的地国家概况... 80
Part Five Consolidation
第五部分：巩固练习... 82

Chapter 7 观光娱乐 — 85
Sightseeing and Recreation

Part One Case Study
第一部分：案例分析... 86
Part Two Listening Comprehension
第二部分：听力训练... 88
Part Three Situational Dialogue
第三部分：情景对话... 89
Part Four ABC about Destination Countries
第四部分：目的地国家概况... 94
Part Five Consolidation
第五部分：巩固练习... 96

Chapter 8 购物与自由活动 — 99
Shopping and Free Activities

Part One Case Study
第一部分：案例分析... 100
Part Two Listening Comprehension
第二部分：听力训练... 102
Part Three Situational Dialogue
第三部分：情景对话... 103
Part Four ABC about Destination Countries
第四部分：目的地国家概况... 110
Part Five Consolidation
第五部分：巩固练习... 112

Chapter 9 安全与应急处理 — 115
Security and Emergencies

Part One Case Study
第一部分：案例分析... 116
Part Two Listening Comprehension
第二部分：听力训练... 117
Part Three Situational Dialogue
第三部分：情景对话... 119
Part Four ABC about Destination Countries
第四部分：目的地国家概况... 121

Part Five Consolidation
第五部分：巩固练习...123

Chapter 10 离境回国 ■127
Departure from Destination Countries

Part One Case Study
第一部分：案例分析...128

Part Two Listening Comprehension
第二部分：听力训练...130

Part Three Situational Dialogue
第三部分：情景对话...131

Part Four ABC about Destination Countries
第四部分：目的地国家概况...134

Part Five Consolidation
第五部分：巩固练习...136

Chapter 1

出团前的准备
Preparations Before Departure

Learning Focus 学习要点

- ◆ **Case Study**
  Annoyance from Pre-departure Briefing
- ◆ **Listening Comprehension**
  Tips for Tour Leader Before Departure
- ◆ **Situational Dialogue**
  Task 1-1 Preparations Before Going Abroad
  　　　　—Visa Application
  Task 1-2 Contact the Local Guide
  　　　　—Confirming Tourists' Information
  Task 1-3 Pre-departure Briefing
  　　　　—ABC about Tourist Behavior
  Task 1-4 Transfer Formalities with the Tour Operator
  　　　　—Transferring Necessary Formalities
  Task 1-5 Taboos for the Tour Leader
  　　　　—Instructions from the Manager Before Departure
- ◆ **ABC about Destination Countries**
  ABC about Singapore
- ◆ **Consolidation**
  Practical Writing: Invitation for Pre-departure Briefing
  Translation for Tour Leader

- ◆ 案例分析
  行前说明会带来的烦恼
- ◆ 听力训练
  领队离境准备建议
- ◆ 情景对话
  ①出国前的准备
  ——申请签证
  ②联系地陪
  ——确认游客信息
  ③行前说明会
  ——游客行为举止知识
  ④与计调交接
  ——交接相关手续
  ⑤领队带团禁忌
  ——经理行前谈话
- ◆ 目的地国家概况
  新加坡概况
- ◆ 巩固练习
  应用文写作：行前说明会邀请函
  领队翻译

Part One Case Study
第一部分：案例分析

Annoyance from Pre-departure Briefing
行前说明会带来的烦恼

An international travel service had a packaged tour for 30 tourists to the United Arab Emirates. The tour leader should have made a pre-departure briefing and operated in accordance with the requirements of The Travel Service Quality for Outbound Tourism. As an experienced tour leader, he often took groups around the world, so he thought it was unnecessary to have a pre-departure briefing. Instead, he planned to conduct the briefing at the airport where he could speak to all of them. However, the tourists arrived at the airport from different places at different times, so he had to hurriedly make a simple and short briefing to them respectively.

After he introduced the related matters the tour leader handed out the relevant materials to the tourists. Being busy with check-in, he had no time to explain the details to Mr. Huang who arrived late. It was not until they reached the destination country that he gave him the travel schedule, talking briefly about the travel tips.

Mr. Huang traveled abroad for the first time. Being curious, he took pictures of the local women with veils without getting their permission. It was a serious offence, and a conflict with local residents happened. He was beaten and injured. Consequently, he had to fly home earlier. Back in China, Mr. Huang requested the travel service to do an apology, reimburse his medical expenses and compensate for his emotional distress because the tour leader didn't tell him the notice to visitors in the destination country before departure.

 扫一扫，看译文。

1. Study the case carefully. Decide whether the following statements are true or false and write T for true and F for false.

(1) Because the tour leader often took groups abroad, it was not necessary to have a briefing.

(2) The tourists arrived at the airport at different time, so the tour leader had to make simple and short briefings to different groups at different time.

(3) The tourists could take pictures of the Arab women with veils in the public.

Chapter 1

出团前的准备
Preparations Before Departure

 扫一扫，有答案。

2. Divide the class into several groups for a brief discussion. One student makes a presentation of the main points and the others give comments on the presentation.

Discussions:

(1) How would you handle the case if you were a tour leader?

(2) Try to put forward more suggestions to the tour leader who is handling the cultural conflict.

① _____
② _____
③ _____
④ _____
⑤ _____

 扫一扫，有答案。

 小知识

领队出团前的准备

领队出发前，应当准备好以下与出团相关的各种资料、表格和物品，以备境外带团使用：

1. 游客情况一览表：注明团队成员基本信息和必要联系方式，如电话号码等。
2. 境外住房名单表：对于散客应考虑单位、年龄、职位等综合因素进行分房。
3. 团队行程计划：如有必要，可与前往国家接待社的地陪确认行程计划。
4. 前往国家(地区)海关申报表：预先准备此表，以方便游客出入境申报物品。
5. 联系人电话表：前往国家接待社经理、地陪的联系方式和组团社责任人的联系方式。
6. 护照、签证、机票、导游旗等。
7. 个人生活用品：药品、雨具、洗漱用品等。

Part Two Listening Comprehension
第二部分：听力训练

Words and Expressions

destination	n.	目的地，终点	transfer	v.	迁移，移交
surname	n.	姓	luggage	n.	行李
currency	n.	货币，通货	procedure	n.	手续，程序

Tips for the Tour Leader Before Departure
领队离境准备建议

1. Listen to the passage and fill in the blanks with the missing information.

 扫一扫，听一听。

Advise the tour leader to (1) _____. The tour leaders takes all of these to the counter. The agent wants to know (2) _____ and the exact number of bags (check-in bags) (3) _____.

It is a good idea to check luggage through to the final destination if you have to change flights since it saves (4) _____.

Take the luggage tags correctly, and write down the names of tourists (5) _____ and keep them properly. When the tour leaders receives the boarding passes, advise the tour leaders to sort them out and (6) _____.

Advise the tourists to change some Renminbi (yuan) to US dollars or (7) _____ after the check-in procedure is done.

 扫一扫，有答案。

2. Listen to the passage again, and try to summarize the suggestions in your own words.

Part Three Situational Dialogue
第三部分：情景对话

Words and Expressions

emergency	n.	紧急情况	reserve	v.	预留，保留
confirm	v.	确认	shameful	adj.	不体面的
haggle	v.	讨价还价	intrusion	n.	打扰
formality	n.	手续	vaccination	n.	接种疫苗
first aid		紧急救护	negotiate	v.	协商
log	n.	日志	taboo	n.	禁忌

Task 1-1 Preparations Before Going Abroad 出国前的准备

Visa Application 申请签证

1. Listen to the dialogue and write numbers in the blanks to show the correct order of the conversation.

扫一扫，听一听。

(C=Clerk; T=Tour Leader)

____ (1) **C:** when will you leave?

____ (2) **T:** Yes, I'm a tour leader of the International Travel Agency. I'd like to apply for 30 visas in my group. Here are the passports.

____ (3) **C:** Good morning, sir. What can I do for you?

____ (4) **T:** Just on this Friday.

____ (5) **C:** OK. Where will you go? And what's your travel plan?

____ (6) **T:** We are going to Paris for one week. We have reserved flight tickets and hotels, and we also have the detailed plan.

____ (7) **C:** Congratulations. Have a nice trip!

____ (8) **C:** Have you been a tour leader before? Do you know what you will do in case of emergencies?

____ (9) **T:** Of course. I have been a tour leader for 5 years and I know much about it.

扫一扫，有答案。

2. Listen to the dialogue again, and act it out with your deskmate. Pay attention to your body language.

Task 1-2 Contact the Local Guide 联系地陪

Confirming Tourists' Information 确认游客信息

1. Listen to the dialogue and fill in blanks with the missing words or phrases you've just heard.

 扫一扫，听一听。

(T=Tour Leader;   L=Local guide)

L: Hello. ABC Travel Service. Sally speaking. May I help you?

T: Yes, this is Wu Jiayi in CITS. I'd like to (1) _____.

L: OK, Ms. Wu Jiayi. Let me see. You told me you would come to New York (2) _____ _____. Are there any big changes?

T: No, but we need (3) _____. Would you please make a reservation for us?

L: Yes, of course. (4)_____.

T: Thank you very much. I am going to send by e-mail the name lists and guests' information. Would you please (5)_____?

L: That' great. Thank you very much.

T: It's my pleasure.

 扫一扫，有答案。

2. Listen to the dialogue again and choose the most courteous expression suitable to the situation from the choices.

(T=Tour Leader ;   L=Local guide)

L: Hello. I am Sally. Who are you?
A. Hello. This is sally speaking. Can I help you?
B. Hello. I am Sally. What can I do for you?
C. Hello. Sally's speaking. What's your name?

T: I am Wu Jiayi in CITS. I want to confirm information with you.
A. Yes. I am Wu Jiayi in CITS. I need your help to confirm guests' information.

Chapter 1

出团前的准备
Preparations Before Departure

B. Yes. I am Wu Jiayi in CITS. Would you mind confirming guests' information with me?

C. Yes. This is Wu Jiayi in CITS. I hope you can confirm guest's information with me.

L: OK, Ms.Wu Jiayi. No problem.

A. OK, Wu Jiayi. I'd like to.

B. Sure, Wu Jiayi. I'd love to solve the problem for you.

C. Sure, Ms.Wu Jiayi. Willing to work for you.

T: We have a group of 30 members. Do you know that?

A. Thank you for your cooperation. We have a group of 30 members. Are you sure of that?

B. Many Thanks. We have a group of 30 members. Have you kept it in mind?

C. Thanks. We have a group of 30 members. I need your reconfirmation.

L: I need you to reconfirm the information.

A. Would you please reconfirm the information?

B. Your reconfirmation is needed.

C. You should have reconfirmed the information.

 扫一扫，有答案。

Task 1-3 Pre-departure Briefing 行前说明会

ABC about Tourist Behavior 游客行为举止小知识

1. Listen to the dialogue and answer the following questions.

 扫一扫，听一听。

(1) What kind of behaviors is regarded as a shameful one?
_____

(2) What should we do when we go shopping?
_____

(3) What questions should we avoid asking the local people?
_____

 扫一扫，有答案。

7

2. Listen to the dialogue again and discuss with your group about what we should do when we travel in London.

Task 1-4 Transfer Formalities with the Tour Operator 与计调交接

Transferring Necessary Formalities 交接相关手续

1. Listen to the dialogue and write down the relevant information you've heard.

 扫一扫，听一听。

(1) The trip to the United States has been scheduled. I have collected and _____ _____. May I transfer them to you?

(2) That's all right. Now, let's check the documents. Here are the name list of the guests, their passports, visas and _____.

(3) You'd better copy all of these documents and _____ in case of being lost or stolen.

(4) Here is the itinerary. You need to bear it in mind. If the local guide changes it at random, you have to _____.

(5) Please check the form of the name list. Keep it carefully with you. You need it when you __ _____.

(6) The last are airplane tickets. Please check the information of electronic tickets to ensure that all guests' names are _____.

(7) Would you please sign your name on this form, which means you've confirmed and _____ _____?

(8) By the way, it is very important to keep the log _____.

 扫一扫，有答案。

2. Role play: One student plays the role of the tour leader while another plays the role of the operator who is transferring the documents and necessary formalities.

Chapter 1

出团前的准备
Preparations Before Departure

Task 1-5 Taboos for the Tour Leader 领队带团禁忌

Instructions from the Manager Before Departure 经理行前谈话

1. Listen to the dialogue and fill in blanks with the missing words or phrases you've just heard.

 扫一扫，听一听。

(T=Tour Leader; M=Manager)

M: Hello, Wu Jiayi. Do you have time?

T: Of course.

M: Last time, I suggested something you should pay attention to about the trip. Here, I would like to share with you other important issues.

T: Great, (1)_____ was really helpful. I would like to learn more.

M: OK, you need to pay attention to (2)_____, try your best to (3)_____ and make them clear of conventions, regulations, (4)_____.

T: I'll try my best to make every tourist comfortable.

M: Good, you'd better not (5)_____ when you return. Are you clear?

T: Yes, of course. I will take care of everything.

M: OK. If everything is fine, I will see you in ten days. But most importantly, ensure every guest will (6)_____.

T: I understand.

 扫一扫，有答案。

2. Discussion: Role play this dialogue with your partner, and discuss if there are other taboos that the tour leader should introduce to the tourists.

Part Four ABC about Destination Countries
第四部分：目的地国家概况

Singapore 新加坡

Singapore, officially the Republic of Singapore, became independent from Malaysia on 9th August, 1965. Then it has been a sovereign (主权), democratic and independent state. The nation of immigrants, including the local, Chinese, Malays, Indians, Europeans and Americans, has its multi-culture. So to promote racial harmony is the core policy of the government.

Singapore is not just one island but a main island with 63 surrounding islets(小岛). The main island has a total land area of 682 square km. In just 150 years, Singapore has grown into a thriving centre of commerce and industry. Its former role as an entrepot (集散地) has diminished, as the Republic has increased its manufacturing (制造) base. It has also become one of the most important financial centres of Asia, with more than 130 banks.

The country of Singapore is also a city, which is known as the Garden City. The Singapore River flows across the city, whose banks are the first choice for immigrants. At the estuary of the river stands the "Merlion"(鱼尾狮) made of white stone, which is the most national personification of the Singapore. The famous attractions also include Gardens by the Bay (滨海湾花园), Bukit Timah Nature Reserve (武吉知马自然保护区), Clarke Quay (克拉码头), Geylang Serai (芽笼士乃港湾) and so on.

Singapore is also a paradise of food, owing to its multi-culture and rich history and the cuisines, including Bak kut Teh(肉骨茶), Nasi Lemak(椰浆饭), Laksa(叻沙), Chendol (珍多) and many other dishes, influenced by China, India, and other countries.

Business dealings are facilitated by Singapore's superb communications network which links the Republic to the rest of the world via satellite (卫星), 24-hour telegraph and telephone systems. Singapore's strategic location, excellent facilities, fascinating cultural contrasts and tourist attractions contribute to its success as a leading destination for both business and pleasure.

Read the passage aloud and choose the best answer to complete each statement.

1. Singapore consists of _____.
   A. a main island with 63 surrounding islets   B. an island
   C. 63 surrounding islets   D. 63 islands
2. Which one of the following is the antonym of "diminish" in the passage?
   A. decrease   B. increase   C. minimize   D. lessen
3. Singapore is the busiest port in the world with over 600 shipping lines sending _____.
   A. super tankers   B. passengers liners
   C. container ships   D. All of the above
4. Based on the text, which of the following statements is NOT the reason for Singapore being a leading destination for both business and pleasure?
   A. fascinating cultural contrasts   B. excellent facilities
   C. strategic location   D. top companies

Chapter 1

出团前的准备
Preparations Before Departure

 扫一扫，有答案。

Watch the short video twice, and complete the following requirements.

Step 1: Watch the video and take notes of what you have watched or heard. Compare the notes with your desk mate.

Step 2: Watch the video again and fill in the blanks in the following sentences with what you have watched or heard.

Summary:

1. Singapore is known as Garden City, and Merlion is the _____ personification of the country.

2. It is also known as the Garden City, which combines skyscrapers with a _____ pot of cultures, tropical climate, tasty food, shopping and a vibrant nightlife.

3. Marina Bay is an area surrounding a bay in the southern part of Singapore, a mix-development area that includes commercial, residential, hotel and _____ buildings.

4. Private owners of these historical buildings were encouraged to restore their properties and government constructed a promenade along the river to facilitate _____ movement.

5. Orchard Road is where tourists can do all their _____, and many local people come here to shop.

 扫一扫，看视频。

Part Five Consolidation
第五部分：巩固练习

Practical Writing 应用文写作

Invitation for Pre-departure Briefing
行前说明会邀请函

All tourists who will be joining the tour group are invited to attend the Briefing. The Briefing will be conducted by the tour leader of the travel service. This is an opportunity

11

for tourists to ask questions and to be informed of important issues before leaving for the destination.

Suppose you are the tour leader, write out a notice for a pre-departure briefing according to the outline given below. Pay attention to the format of the invitation.

Outline:

(1) Time for the briefing: 3:00 p.m. August 3rd, 2013

(2) Place: the multi-functional meeting room of the Travel Service

(3) Content: Pre-departure briefing and the importance of the briefing

(4) Participants: tourists who have joined the trip

 扫一扫，有答案。

Translation for the Tour Leader 领队翻译

1. Translate the following sentences into English with the words or phrases given.

(1) 领队应在行前说明会上介绍旅行细节、分发(distribute)资料。

(2) 请注意： 如果您不参加旅游，将承担(bear)各项实际发生的一切费用。

(3) 我代表中国国际旅行社和我们的司机，向大家表示最热烈的欢迎。

(4) 我随团(tourist group)旅行。吴佳仪女士是我们团的领队。

(5) 领队应该接受任务，了解(get acquainted with)团队情况，熟悉案卷和接待计划。

 扫一扫，做翻译。

2. Translate the following sentences into Chinese with the words or phrases given.

(1) When escorting the outbound tourists, a tour leader may sometimes meet some tourists who complain unreasonably because of their own bad manners. The tour leader should be neither humble or arrogant(不卑不亢).

(2) The possession of a passport is essential for an outbound travel.

(3) "R", the first letter stands for (代表) "ready" which shows that the tour leader is constantly ready to serve tourists.

(4) I've already applied for passports for my 15 distinguished guests (贵宾).

(5) People think that I'm bilingual(双语的). They think that I know about everything in the world. If I am going to take a group to foreign countries, I should have got to know all the facts and the figures.

扫一扫，做翻译。

本章参考文献

[1]曹景洲.海外旅游领队业务[M].北京：中国旅游出版社，2011.
[2]曹银玲.出境领队实务[M].北京：旅游教育出版社，2012.
[3]黄恢月，仉向明.出境旅游领队工作案例解析[M].北京：旅游教育出版社，2008.
[4]王远梅.空乘英语[M].北京：国防工业出版社，2010.
[5]王健民.出境旅游领队实务[M].5版.北京：旅游教育出版社，2016.
[6]袁智敏，仉向明.领队英语[M].2版.北京：旅游教育出版社，2008.
[7]张明清，窦志萍.导游服务案例选——技巧与提高[M].昆明：云南大学出版社，2007.
[8]朱歧新.英语导游必读[M].北京：中国旅游出版社，2005.
[9]https://www.csair.com/cn/index.shtml
[10]http://travel.state.gov/
[11]http://www.outbound-tourism.cn/
[12]http://www.ppinpoint.com/

Chapter 2

中国出境
Departure from China

Learning Focus　学习要点

- ◆ **Case Study**
  An Old Lady Halted by Security Check
- ◆ **Listening Comprehension**
  Boarding the Plane
- ◆ **Situational Dialogue**
  Task 2-1　Airport Check-in
  　　　　　—At the Information Desk
  Task 2-2　Luggage Check-in
  　　　　　—Luggage Missing
  　　　　　—Luggage Misplaced
  　　　　　—Luggage Check-in
  Task 2-3　Ready for Boarding
  　　　　　—Airport Announcements
  　　　　　—Boarding Gate
- ◆ **ABC about Destination Countries**
  ABC about the United Kingdom
- ◆ **Consolidation**
  Practical Writing: Memorandum
  Translation for Tour Leader

- ◆ 案例分析
  老太太过安检受阻
- ◆ 听力训练
  登机
- ◆ 情景对话
  ①办理机场登机手续
  ——在问讯处
  ②托运行李
  ——行李丢失
  ——行李错挂
  ——行李托运
  ③准备登机
  ——机场广播
  ——登机门
- ◆ 目的地国家概况
  英国概况
- ◆ 巩固练习
  应用文写作：备忘录
  领队翻译

Part One Case Study
第一部分：案例分析

An Old Lady Halted by Security Check
老太太过安检受阻

On the Labor's Day Miss. Lv Mengsha, an outbound tour leader took a group of 32 tourists to Australia to have a 7-day tour. They went through the security check at Shanghai Pudong International Airport. Unexpectedly, the contraband got them into trouble: an old lady who suffered from rheumatism brought 7 bottles of Chinese liquid herbal medicine with her. An airport security officer asked her to present the doctor's prescription, but she couldn't provide any. She said repeatedly the medicine was very important to her health and the tour leader didn't say anything about the contraband before the trip. At last, the officer asked the tour leader to take the lady to airport service counter to have the medicine checked and registered. Eventually, one bottle of medicine was allowed to be taken aboard while others were not allowed. The old lady became seriously ill when she traveled aboard. Back in China, she made a complaint against the tour leader and the travel service.

 扫一扫，看译文。

1. Study the case carefully. Decide whether the following statements are true or false and write T for true and F for false.

(1) _____ The outbound tour leader got into trouble because tourists took with them traditional Chinese herbal medicines.

(2) _____ 7 bottles of Chinese liquid herbal medicine were registered as contraband goods.

(3) _____ The tour leader should be held responsible for the old lady's illness and should pay her for the medical expenses.

 扫一扫，有答案。

16

Chapter 2
中国出境
Departure from China

2. Divide the class into several groups for a brief discussion. One student makes a presentation of the main points discussed and the others give comments on the presentation.

Discussions:

(1) What should the tour leader do to discourage the tourists from taking with them the contraband goods?

(2) Try to put forward more suggestions to the tour leader.

① _____

② _____

③ _____

④ _____

⑤ _____

 扫一扫，议一议。

 小知识

办理出境口岸手续

1. 领队须在规定时间、规定地点等候游客，提醒游客提前做好申报准备，申报物品不要放在托运行李内。
2. 清点人数，联系未到团友，确认其位置，催促其到达。
3. 交纳国际机场建设费(或客人自理)，12岁以下儿童免交。
4. 指导需办理海关申报的游客走红色通道，其他游客走绿色通道。
5. 前往指定柜台，清点行李数，统一办理登机手续，办理行李托运，检查登机牌。
6. 分发登机牌，提醒登机口和登机时间。
7. 过卫生检疫，出示黄皮书或购药的发票。提醒游客注意一米线，尊重现场工作人员。
8. 过边检时，按出境名单顺序通过，名单上没有的客人须填写出境卡。
9. 出境名单存收两份，边检存一份。
10. 带领游客过安检、候机、登机。

Part Two Listening Comprehension
第二部分：听力训练

Words and Expressions

prior	adj.	优先的	attendant	n.	服务人员
designate	v.	标明	buildup	n.	集结
stow	v.	装，装载	luxury	n.	奢华

Boarding the Plane 登机

1. Listen to the passage and fill in the blanks with the missing information.

 扫一扫，听一听。

(1) **Wait for the announcement to board.** About half an hour prior to takeoff, the flight attendant will ①_____. Boarding is done in sections, either by group/sections (designated with a letter) or by rows/seats. Check your boarding pass to see if you ②_____, and if not, wait for your row or a section of rows to be called.

(2) **Get your boarding pass checked.** After waiting in line for boarding, there will be a flight attendant next to the entrance ③_____. Keep your boarding pass out after having it checked, as you may need to show it to another flight attendant on the plane.

(3) **Enter the aircraft.** There is typically a buildup of passengers after the boarding pass check, so you may have to wait in line again before boarding the plane. Check your seat to make sure you are ④_____, and keep a lookout for your row number.

(4) **Stow your carry-on items.** When you have located your seat, place your smaller bag on your chair, and look for available space in the overhead bins for ⑤_____
_____.

(5) **Get settled in.** You're all done! Now it's time for you to ⑥_____
_____ while you are carried away to your destination in luxury.

 扫一扫，有答案。

18

Chapter 2
中国出境
Departure from China

2. Listen to the dialogue about boarding the plane and try to answer the following questions.

(1) When will the flight attendant announce the boarding time?
_____

(2) Why do you need to keep your boarding pass out after having it checked?
_____

(3) Why do you have to wait in line before boarding the plane?
_____

 扫一扫，有答案。

Part Three Situational Dialogue
第三部分：情景对话

Words and Expressions

booth	n.	电话亭	upstairs	adv.	在楼上
claim tag		行李单	escalator	n.	自动扶梯
terminal	n.	航站楼	maintenance	n.	维修，保养
exceed	v.	超出	typhoon	n.	台风
refrain	v.	禁止	compensation	n.	赔偿

Task 2-1 Airport Check-in 办理机场登机手续

At the Information Desk 在问讯处

1. Listen to the dialogue and put the following responses in the correct order.

 扫一扫，听一听。

Clerk	Tour Leader
(1) Good afternoon, madam. May I help you?	A: 1:30 p.m.
(2) Go down to the far end of the lounge and you'll find the counter for flights to Tokyo.	B: Could you tell me where I check in for the Flight NH 203 to Tokyo?
(3) What is the departure time of your flight?	C: Thanks.

19

	续表
(4) Let me see. It's 11:00 a.m. now. So they will start in about an hour.	D: Do you know when they begin to check in?
(5) You'll find phone booths upstairs, madam.	E: Thank you very much. By the way, where can I make a phone call?
(6) It's my pleasure.	

 扫一扫，有答案。

2. Pair work: Listen to the dialogue again, repeat it sentence by sentence, and then role-play it in pairs.

Task 2-2 Luggage Check-in 托运行李

Luggage Missing 行李丢失

1. Listen to the dialogue and fill in the blanks with the information you hear.

 扫一扫，听一听。

(T=Tang Ying, Tour Leader; S= Stewardess; C= Chen Ling, Tourist)

T: Excuse me, miss.

S: Yes, may I help you?

T: I'm **Tang Ying**, the tour leader of CITS. One of our group members left his briefcase (1)_____at the airport.

S: If you can give me a description, I'll ask our ground personnel to try to locate it for you.

C: It's a (2)_____with baggage claim tags. It has my name on it too—Chen Ling. It also has my address in Hangzhou. I'll need it in Switzerland. It contains some important business papers.

S: Are you sure you left it in the departure lounge?

C: Yes, I'm sure now. When our flight was announced, I left it (3)_____. I had just bought a carton to take with me on the trip.

S: I'm quite sure we can find it then. Can you give me the name of your hotel?

T: Yes. We'll be staying at the Genevese Hilton Hotel (4)_____.

S: We'll probably get it on tomorrow's flight. When it arrives in Geneva, we'll contact you at Hilton.

T: Thank you, Miss. I really appreciate your help. We'll write down (5)_____with the name of our hotel and the exact dates we'll be staying there.

S: My pleasure.

 扫一扫，有答案。

2. Listen to the dialogue again and perform it without looking at the books. Discuss with your partner about the alternative expressions.

(1) Explain the problem.

(2) Describe the luggage.

(3) Give the name and address.

(4) Show appreciation.

Luggage Misplaced 行李错挂

1. Listen to the dialogue and answer the following questions.

 扫一扫，听一听。

(1) Where shall we go if we can't find our luggage in the luggage claim area?

_____

(2) What kind of luggage did the tourist lose?

_____

(3) How to deal with the problem if the luggage is damaged?

_____

 扫一扫，有答案。

2. Group work: role play with your partners according to the following setting.

Two actors: A. clerk of the airline B. tour leader

Some of your group members tell you that they can't find their luggage (2 big black backpacks and 1 small grey leather case). But these tourists can't speak English, so you help them to communicate with the clerks.

More information: FLT.No. SQ368 to Singapore. The luggage is misplaced on Flight KA217.

Luggage Check-in 行李托运

1. Listen to the dialogue and write numbers in the blanks to show the correct order of the conversation.

 扫一扫，听一听。

(C= Clerk; T= Tour Leader)

_____ (1) **C:** I'm afraid not. It's overweight. One piece of carry-on baggage may not exceed limit of 5 kg.

_____ (2) **T:** Thank you very much.

_____ (3) **T:** I see.

_____ (4) **T:** Yes, we're here to check in for the flight to Sydney. Here are our tickets and passports.

_____ (5) **C:** May I help you, sir?

_____ (6) **T:** Twenty pieces altogether. Can I take this traveling bag as a carry-on?

_____ (7) **C:** Thank you, sir. Please put your baggage on the scale. How many pieces of baggage do you want to check in?

_____ (8) **C:** Here are twenty claim tags for your baggage and your passports.

 扫一扫，有答案。

2. Listen to the dialogue again, and act it out with your deskmate.

Task 2-3 Ready for Boarding 准备登机

Airport Announcements 机场广播

1. Listen to the dialogue carefully and fill in the table with correct information.

扫一扫，听一听。

The number of the delayed flight:	
The reason for delay:	
When is the plane scheduled to depart?	
When will the plane depart?	

22

Chapter **2**

中国出境
Departure from China

 扫一扫，有答案。

2. Listen to the announcements and put the following responses in the correct order.

 扫一扫，听一听。

(1) Commencement of Boarding

(2) Delay Due to Maintenance

(3) Cancellations

(4) Commencement of Check-in

(5) Final Boarding Call

 扫一扫，有答案。

Boarding Gate 登机门

1. Listen to the dialogue and fill in the blanks with the information you hear.

 扫一扫，听一听。

　　(T=Traveler; C=Clerk)

T: Excuse me, I am going to take (1)_____, can you tell me where my boarding gate is?

C: Let me see your ticket. OK, your flight is boarding (2)_____.

T: Thanks. But would you please tell me (3)_____?

C: Just go down the escalator and take the tram to the domestic terminal. Turn left (4)_____ and follow the signs to your gate.

 扫一扫，有答案。

2. Pair work: Listen to the dialogue again, repeat it sentence by sentence, and then role-play it in pairs.

23

Part Four ABC about Destination Countries
第四部分：目的地国家概况

The United Kingdom 英国

The United Kingdom of Great Britain and Northern Ireland, or UK lies between the North Atlantic Ocean (大西洋) and the North Sea, and comes within 35 km (22 miles) of the northwest coast of France, from which it is separated by the English Channel (英吉利海峡). It comprises the island of Great Britain (England, Scotland and Wales) and the northeastern one-sixth of the island of Ireland (Northern Ireland), together with many smaller islands. The United Kingdom has a total area of approximately 245,000 square kilometers.

The United Kingdom is a constitutional monarchy with a parliamentary democracy and its capital city is London. Great Britain, the dominant industrial and maritime power of the 19th century, played a leading role in developing parliamentary democracy (议会民主制)and in advancing literature and science. At its zenith (顶峰), the British Empire Stretched over one-fourth of the earth's surface.

Historically, indigenous British people were thought to be descended from the various ethnic groups that settled there before the 11th century: the Celts (凯尔特人), Romans, Anglo-Saxons(盎格鲁-撒克逊人), Norse (挪威人) and the Normans (诺曼人). Welsh (威尔士人) people could be the oldest ethnic group in the UK. The UK has a history of small-scale non-white immigration, with Liverpool having the oldest black population in the country dating back to at least the 1730s during the period of the African slave trade. The UK also has the oldest Chinese community in Europe, dating to the arrival of Chinese seamen (水手) in the 19th century. In 2016, 31.4% of primary and 27.9% of secondary pupils at state schools in England were members of an ethnic minority.

Forms of Christianity (基督教) have dominated religious life in what is now the United Kingdom for over 1400 years. But immigration and demographic change have contributed to the growth of other faiths, most notably Islam, which lead the UK described as a multi-faith, secularised, or post-Christian society. For tourists, the Church of England ranks one of the top places to go.

It is well-known that the UK has rich tourism resources, attributing to its history, religion and culture. Besides the capital city London, if you want to experience the traditional British style of its architecture and customs, Windsor (温莎), Eton (伊顿), Oxford (牛津), and Cambridge (剑桥) must be the best. If you have a fond of mediaeval cities (中古小城), the Bath (巴斯), York(约克) and Winchester (温彻斯特) are worthy of going. And if you just snatch leisure from a busy life and want to have a good holiday, you cannot miss the Windermere (温德米尔) and Grasmere (格拉斯米尔).

You can't fail to be excited by London's amazing attractions. See the city from above on the London Eye (伦敦眼); meet a celebrity at Madame Tussaud (杜莎夫人蜡像馆); examine the world's most precious treasures at the British Museum (大英博物馆) or come face-to-face with dinosaurs at the Natural History Museum (自然历史博物馆).

From the modern London Eye, to the historic Tower of London, the top 10 tourist attractions in London are a must-see on any London sightseeing trip. Even better, many London landmarks are free to visit, while others are available with discounted entry or special offers when using a London Pass (伦敦一卡通).

There are also plenty of kid-friendly places to visit in London. Get up close and personal with underwater creatures at SEALIFE London Aquarium (伦敦水族馆) or explore the Science Museum (科学博物馆), London's interactive hub of science and technology. Both are perfect for fun family days out in London.

You could also soak up some culture at London museums, visit the Queen at Buckingham Palace (白金汉宫), or take the perfect picture with Big Ben (大本钟).

Read the passage aloud and choose the best answer to complete each statement.

1. The U.K. consists of _____.
    A. England, Scotland , Wales and Northern Ireland
    B. England, Scotland and Northern Ireland
    C. England, Scotland and Wales
    D. Scotland, Wales and Northern Ireland

2. The Channel links the UK with _____.
    A. Switzerland   B. Germany
    C. Italy   D. France

3. Based on the text, which of the following statements is NOT correct?
    A. People prefer to have a leisurely vacation in London, York, Windermere and Winchester.
    B. Tourists can see many buildings in traditional English style in Oxford and Cambridge.
    C. The UK also has the oldest Chinese community in Europe, dating to the 19th century.
    D. York and Winchester used to be mediaeval cities in the United Kingdom.

4. _____ is most well-known museums in London, one of must-see attractions.
    A. Science Museum   B. Madame Tussaud
    C. British Museum   D. Natural History Museum

 扫一扫，有答案。

Watch the short video twice, and complete the following requirements.

Step 1: Watch the video and take notes of what you have watched or heard. Compare the notes with your desk mate.

Step 2: Watch the video again and fill in the blanks in the following sentences with what you have watched or heard.

Summary:

1. England is a great place to visit whether travelers are making their first or umpteenth trip abroad because the language _____ isn't there for English speakers.

2. Brighton on the Sussex coast has been a popular _____ resort which is lined with graceful old Victorian homes.

3. Cambridge is a _____ city about 80 kilometers north of London, the home to Cambridge University.

4. York is a walled city with a rich heritage where the river falls meets the river outs. Plenty of exciting sites compete for visitors' attention as they stroll along the city's _____ streets.

5. One of the most popular places to visit in Stonehenge is a _____ monument found in Wiltshire.

 扫一扫，看视频。

Part Five Consolidation
第五部分：巩固练习

Practical Writing 应用文写作

Memorandum 备忘录

Memo writing is practically a requirement in the company. Memoranda or memos are business messages, which transmit information to those within a company. Memos are a form of internal correspondence for employees. Unlike letters, there is no need to address each individual in the company. Furthermore, as a tour leader, it's necessary to acquire such skills to pass information.

Suppose you are the tour operator Lisa. According to the given information, you need to finish the following memo, and remind Mr. Li to pass the message to Jason who will be back to the company in the afternoon.

Chapter 2

中国出境
Departure from China

Outline:

1. There will be a training course on "How to Help Tourists to Get through Security Check Quickly".

2. The time and date of the course is 3:00 P.M., on September 1st. The place is the First Conference Room.

3. Jason is asked to attend the training course.

4. Lisa's phone number is 12345678901.

```
                              Memo
To: _____
From: _____
Subject: _____




```

Sample:

```
                              Memo
To: Tobby, Tour Operator
From: Wang Jing, Tour Operator
Subject: The Change of Departure Time

    The departure time of "5.1 Tour to Hong Kong, Macao, Taiwan" has changed to 3:00
p.m. 1st, May. Please tell Zhang Jie the change of time, ask him to communicate with
tourists immediately and try to get their understanding and cooperation. Besides, my e-mail
address is touroperator@travel.com. You are welcome to contact me at any time.
```

 扫一扫，有答案。

Translation for the Tour Leader 领队翻译

1. Translate the following sentences into English with the words or phrases given.

(1) 请把您的健康证明和防疫证明(Vaccination Certificate)给我看一下。

(2) 请问在哪里换登机牌？给行李称重(weigh)？

(3) 您可以随身带一件手提行李(hand luggage)上机。

(4) 旅客们请注意，泰国航空公司(Thai Airways)飞往曼谷的454次航班就要起飞了，请乘坐这次航班的旅客到7号门登机。

(5) 您的行李箱需要经过X光(X-ray)检查，贴上验放标签(label)。

 扫一扫，做翻译。

2. Translate the following sentences into Chinese with the words or phrases given.

(1) Please go through one by one according to the order of the name list (名单).

(2) Is this check-in counter for taking Flight NH (全日空) 203 to Tokyo?

(3) Which belt (传送带) is for the baggage form Flight BA 328?

(4) Your baggage exceeds the free baggage allowance(限额).

(5) Go down the escalator at the end of the hallway, and the baggage claim is on your right.

 扫一扫，做翻译。

本章参考文献

[1]曹景洲. 海外旅游领队业务[M]. 北京：中国旅游出版社, 2011.

[2]曹银玲. 出境领队实务[M]. 北京：旅游教育出版社, 2012.

[3]黄恢月，仉向明. 出境旅游领队工作案例解析[M]. 北京：旅游教育出版社, 2008.

[4]王远梅. 空乘英语[M]. 北京：国防工业出版社, 2010.

[5]王健民. 出境旅游领队实务[M]. 5版. 北京：旅游教育出版社, 2016.

[6]袁智敏，仉向明. 领队英语[M]. 2版. 北京：旅游教育出版社, 2008.

[7]张明清，窦志萍. 导游服务案例选——技巧与提高[M]. 昆明：云南大学出版社, 2007.

[8]朱歧新. 英语导游必读[M]. 北京：中国旅游出版社, 2005.

[9]https://www.csair.com/cn/index.shtml

[10]http://travel.state.gov/

[11]http://www.outbound-tourism.cn/

[12]http://www.visitlondon.com/things-to-do/visiting-london-for-the-first-time/ten-reasons-to-visit-london#cOBTXi2PcdrHEO8g.97

Chapter 3

飞行途中
On the Flight

Learning Focus 学习要点

◆ **Case Study**
   A Theft During the Flight

◆ **Listening Comprehension**
   A Bulkhead Seat

◆ **Situational Dialogue**
   Task 3-1 In-flight Service
         —Asking for Chinese Newspaper
         —Asking for Change of Seats
         —Inquiries about In-flight Facilities
   Task 3-2 In-flight Meals
         —Ordering Main Course
         —Asking for a Refill of Soft Drink
   Task 3-3 Taking Care of the Sick Tourists
         —Asking for Blankets
         —Beating Jet Lag
   Task 3-4 Preparations Before Landing
         —Inquires about Ground Information
         —Inquires about Destination

◆ **ABC about Destination Countries**
   ABC about Canada

◆ **Consolidation**
   Practical Writing: Arrival Form /Entry Form
   Translation for Tour Leader

◆ 案例分析
   机上盗窃案
◆ 听力训练
   紧急通道座位
◆ 情景对话
   ①机上服务
      ——索要中文报纸
      ——要求换座位
      ——询问机上设备
   ②机上就餐
      ——点主菜
      ——要求加软饮料
   ③照看身体不适的游客
      ——要求加毛毯
      ——倒时差
   ④飞机着陆前的准备
      ——询问地面情况
      ——询问目的地情况
◆ 目的地国家概况
   加拿大概况
◆ 巩固练习
   应用文写作：出入境表
   领队翻译

Part One Case Study
第一部分：案例分析

A Theft During the Flight 机上盗窃案

On the flight from Beijing to San Francisco, a thief on board pretended to be a tourist and disguised himself among tour members. He sat beside a tourist and began to talk with him. At first, the tourist didn't talk much, but the thief could always find some topics to chat, gradually the tourist stayed less alert and began to chat with that thief like old friends, and the thief got to know more about the tourist from their conversation. When the plane stopped ascending and reached the cruising altitude, the tourist began to take a nap. At this moment, the thief pretended to open his own baggage looking for something while he secretly opened the tourist's baggage. After searching for a while, he stole 8000 yuan in cash and a valuable camera. Luckily, another tourist happened to witness the process, but he didn't say any words until the plane reached the destination. When the thief was leaving, the witness caught the thief, while asking the stewardess to call the police. After investigation, police found that he was a petty thief, often committing crimes on the plane.

 扫一扫，看译文。

1. Study the case carefully. Decide whether the following statements are true or false and write T for true and F for false.

(1) _____ All the passengers are friends when they are aboard the plane.

(2) _____ In order to kill the time, the tour members can talk about any topics they like with other passengers.

(3) _____ It is quite safe when you are abroad because the flight attendants is around and will take care of your personal properties.

(4) _____ If the tour members lose their carry-on luggage or valuables aboard they can gain some compensation from the airline.

(5) _____ The tour leader is not to blame for the loss of any personal valuables aboard because he is not the air policeman.

 扫一扫，有答案。

Chapter 3
飞行途中
On the Flight

2. Divide the class into several groups for a brief discussion. One student makes a presentation of the main points discussed and the others give comments on the presentation.

Discussions: What could the tour leader do to avoid the possible theft aboard?

Comments:

(1)_____

(2)_____

(3)_____

(4)_____

(5)_____

 扫一扫，有答案。

 小知识

飞行途中领队的工作

旅游的空中飞行时间通常较长，一般少则一两个小时，多则数小时，甚至10多个小时，领队应充分利用机上的时间，熟悉团队。在这段时间内，领队可以做的事情包括：

(1)再次预习接待计划，对游览城市之间的衔接、转换尤其需特别注意。

(2)拿出资料、相关书籍，预习行程中不熟悉的城市和旅游景点。

(3)及时记录出境时发生的问题。

(4)与游客交谈，融洽关系。

(5)为游客提供乘机诸项帮助和服务。如协助游客调换座位，关照游客的特殊用餐要求，熟悉飞机上的救生设备，回答游客的其他提问，帮助游客填写入境表格等。

Part Two Listening Comprehension
第二部分：听力训练

Words and Expressions

bulkhead	n.	隔板	armrest	n.	扶手
partition	n.	分开；隔墙	adjust	v.	调整
section	n.	部分	automatically	adv.	自动地
recline	v.	斜倚	complicated	adj.	复杂的
legroom	n.	放脚的空间	monitor	n.	监视器
stow	v.	装载	destination	n.	目的地

31

1. Listen to the passage and fill in the blanks with the missing information.

扫一扫，听一听。

A Bulkhead Seat 紧急通道座位

A bulkhead is the physical partition that (1) _____ a plane into different classes or sections. Bulkhead seats are the seats located directly behind the bulkhead separators. With no seat in front of you, no one can **recline** (2) _____. This usually makes it easier to enter and exit your seat during flight too. Some bulkhead seats provide (3) _____. If the bulkhead wall is situated very far (4) _____, those sitting in the bulkhead seats will enjoy extra space. In other instances, the bulkhead wall does not reach all the way to the floor, (5) _____.

Cut-outs provide space for you to (6) _____ and sometimes even stow a small carry-on. (Whether or not the Flight Attendants allow you to **store** (7) _____ in the cut-out space is carrier dependent.) While cut-outs differ in size, they are usually no more than a foot high. If you are on an aircraft (8) _____, it may be stored in your seat's armrest because there is no seat back in front of you. Having it come out of the armrest enables you to (9) _____, but may reduce seat width slightly. Some passengers like to put their feet up (10) _____, something that cannot be done when there is a seat in front of you.

扫一扫，有答案。

2. Fill in the blanks with the words and expressions given below. Change their forms when necessary.

bulkhead	divide	partition	recline	stow
adjust	provide	stretch	armrest	carry-on

(1) The personal television may be stored in the seat's _____ .

(2) We recommend that you keep your laptop in your _____ bag when traveling.

(3) Your baggage will be _____ safely away in the plane.

(4) If you are seated uncomfortably, you may try to _____ your seat.

(5) The extra space enables passengers to_____ their legs.
(6) A _____ is designed to separate first class cabin from economy class one.
(7) No passenger _____ into your space, because no seat is in front of you.
(8) The separator has a function of _____ a plane into different classes or sections.
(9) The seat located directly behind the separators _____ the extra space.
(10) The separator is the physical _____ that makes passengers enjoy extra space.

扫一扫，有答案。

Part Three Situational Dialogue
第三部分：情景对话

Words and Expressions

lavatory	n.	盥洗室	airsickness	n.	晕机
vomit	v.	呕吐	turn down		调低
value meal		套餐	chili paste		辣椒酱
beverage	n.	饮料	delay	v.	延迟
take off		起飞	due to		由于
charge	n.	费用	infer	v.	推断

Task 3-1 In-flight Service 机上服务

Asking for Chinese Newspaper 索要中文报纸

1. Listen to the dialogue and write numbers in the brackets to show the correct order of the conversation.

 扫一扫，听一听。

(T=Tour Leader;   S=Stewardess)

_____ S: The lavatories are in the rear of this section, sir.
_____ S: How about *New York Times* and *Washington Post*?
_____ S: Not many, only *People's Daily*. Would you like some copies?
_____ T: Yes, please. That's very kind of you.
_____ T: I see. Thank you, Miss. By the way, have you got something for us to read?

_____ T: Excuse me, Miss, where is the lavatory?

_____ T: I'm sorry. Some tourists of our group can't speak English. Do you have any Chinese newspapers or magazines?

 扫一扫，有答案。

2. Listen to the dialogue again, and act it out with your deskmate. Pay attention to your body language.

Asking for Change of Seats 要求换座位

1. Listen to the dialogue carefully and complete the following sentences in your own words.

 扫一扫，听一听。

(1) Henry asked the tour leader to _____.

(2) The lady needed to change the seat because_____.

(3) The stewardess didn't agree to change the seat at first, because_____.

(4) The tour leader suggested that the stewardess might ask other passenger to _____ _____.

(5) The stewardess asked the lady to hold the airsick bag lest _____.

 扫一扫，有答案。

2. Role play: Act it out with your partner and make dialogue between the stewardess and the passenger who was asked to exchange the seat.

Inquiries about In-flight Facilities 询问机上设备

1. Listen to the dialogue and fill in blanks with what you've just heard.

 扫一扫，听一听。

Chapter 3
飞行途中
On the Flight

(T=Tour Leader;   S=Stewardess)

T: Hello, stewardess.

S: Hello, sir. (1)_____?

T: I feel cold. I want you to turn down the air-conditioner.

S: OK. No problem. (2)_____.

T: Thank you. (3)_____?

S: Look at this. (4)_____.

T: OK. Thank you.

S: What's more?

T: No, thanks.

S: OK.

扫一扫，有答案。

2. Listen to the dialogue again and choose the most courteous expression that is suitable to the situation from the choices below.

(T=Tour Leader; S=Stewardess)

T: I feel cold. I want you to turn down the air-conditioner.

   (1)_____?

A. I feel cold. Could you help me turn down the air-conditioner?

B. I feel cold. Why not turn down the air-conditioner?

C. I feel cold. Help me turn down the air-conditioner.

S: OK. No problem. (2)_____

A. OK, I will adjust the air flow.

B. I'm very sorry to hear that. I will adjust the air flow for you right now.

C. Never mind. I will adjust the air flow.

T: Thank you. (3)_____?

A. Thank you. But you should have turned on the light.

B. Thank you very much. By the way, I am wondering if you can turn on the light for me. I can't find buttons.

C. Turn on the light now! Thank you.

35

S: What's more? (4)_____

A. I'm very busy now.

B. It's my pleasure. Please feel free to call us if you have any questions.

C. This is my duty. Please don't hesitate to call us.

S: OK. (5)_____

A. At your service.

B. That's all right.

C. That's it.

 扫一扫，有答案。

Task 3-2 In-flight Meals 机上就餐

Ordering Main Course 点主菜

1. Listen to the dialogue and put the following responses in the correct order.

 扫一扫，听一听。

Stewardess

(1) It's my pleasure. Enjoy your meal.

(2) Please put down the table in front of you. It's more comfortable that way.

(3) It is beef. Do you like it?

(4) You are welcome. Please press that button if you need any help.

(5) Excuse me, sir. What would you like to have, Chinese food or western food?

(6) OK, enjoy yourself, sir.

Tour Leader

A. Oh, thank you. So nice you are.

B. That's OK. Thanks very much.

C. OK.

D. I'd like to have Chinese food.

E. Thanks a lot. Oh, excuse me. Can I take two value meals? And I want some chili paste.

F. Oh, Sorry to bother you. I want to know what kind of meat it is.

 扫一扫，有答案。

2. Divide the class into groups of two or three students, and do the dialogue again.

Chapter 3
飞行途中
On the Flight

Asking for a Refill of Soft Drink 要求加软饮料

1. Listen to the dialogue and answer the following questions.

 扫一扫，听一听。

(1) What does the guest want to have?
_____

(2) Which beverage is free of charge?
_____

(3) Aside from mineral water, could you list more free beverages?
_____

 扫一扫，有答案。

2. Role play: One student plays the role of the flight attendant while another plays the role of the tour leader who asks for free drinks.

Task 3-3 Taking Care of the Sick Tourists 照看身体不适的游客

Asking for Blankets 要求加毛毯

1. Listen to the dialogue and choose the best answer accordingly.

 扫一扫，听一听。

(1) What is the possible relation between the two speakers?
  A. Husband and wife   B. Teacher and student
  C. Boss and clerk   D. Stewardess and tour leader

(2) What does the man ask for?
  A. airflow   B. blanket
  C. favor   D. help

37

扫一扫，有答案。

2. Listen to the dialogue again, rearrange the order of pictures. Describe the following pictures according to the right order.

_____ _____ _____

 扫一扫，有答案。

Beating Jet Lag 倒时差

1. Listen to the dialogue and match the right picture accordingly.

 扫一扫，听一听。

When did the tourists arrive at New York? What time was it in Beijing? Choose the right picture given below.

A.   B.   C.

 扫一扫，有答案。

Chapter 3
飞行途中
On the Flight

2. Role play: Suppose you are a tour leader and your classmates are tourists from Beijing. Ask the tourists to reset their watch to New York time when they arrive at the destination.

Task 3-4 Preparations Before Landing 飞机着陆前的准备

Inquires about Ground Information 询问地面情况

1. Listen to the dialogue and make some predictions accordingly.

扫一扫，听一听。

(1) According to the dialogue, you are requested to infer the season of Beijing.
   A. Summer　　　　B. Autumn　　　　C. Spring　　　　D. Winter

(2) The first picture shows the ground condition of the destination. If you take flight from Auckland to Beijing, figure out what season it is in Beijing. Choose the correspondent picture from the choices below.

A.

B.

C.

(3) When the guests arrive at Auckland, what is the most suitable clothes for them to wear according to the weather in Auckland? Choose the right one from the following pictures.

A.

B.

C.

39

扫一扫，有答案。

2. Role play: Suppose you are the tour leader, tell the tour members the ground weather conditions before landing.

Inquires about Destination 询问目的地情况

1. Listen to the dialogue and make some predictions accordingly.

 扫一扫，听一听。

(1) According to the dialogue, can you infer the Beijing Time when the tour leader arrives at New York?
   A. 7:50 p.m.   B. 6:50 a.m.   C. 5:50 a.m.   D. 7:40 a.m.

(2) According to the dialogue, the tour leader may have _____ after arrival.
   A. lunch   B. breakfast   C. supper   D. brunch

(3) Tourists arrive at New York on _____ of leaving.
   A. the next day   B. the same day   C. the last day   D. the early day

 扫一扫，有答案。

2. Role play: Suppose you are the guest and the tour leader. Make a dialogue about the weather on the ground before your plane lands the airport.

Part Four ABC about Destination Countries
第四部分：目的地国家概况

Canada 加拿大

Located in the northern part of the North America, Canada is a country consisting of 10 provinces and 3 territories. Extending from the Atlantic(大西洋)to the Pacific(太平洋)and northward into the Arctic Ocean(北冰洋), Canada is the world's second largest country with total area of 9.98 million square kilometers, and its common border with the United States is the world's longest land border shared by two countries. With a population of approximately 35 million, it is one of the world's most ethnically diverse and multicultural nations, the product of large-scale immigration from many countries.

Canada is a federal parliamentary democracy(议会民主制)and a constitutional monarchy(君主立宪制)with Queen Elizabeth II(伊丽莎白二世女王)as its head of state. However, the Queen is primarily figurehead. The real executive power is exercised by the Prime Minister and Cabinet(内阁). The country is officially bilingual(双语)at the federal level. English and French have equal status as official languages. To become a citizen one must be able to speak either English or French.

Canada is a developed country and one of the wealthiest in the world. Relying chiefly upon its abundant natural resources and well-developed trade networks, its economy is one of the largest in the world, with the eighth highest per capita income(人均收入)globally. Canada's long and complex relationship with the United States has had a significant impact on its economy and culture.

As the second largest country in the world with a land mass that covers five time zones, Canada offers plenty of destinations for travelers. Canada has cosmopolitan(大都会) cities and a rich, interesting French heritage(遗产), each offering its own Canadian urban experience, from the laid back charm of Vancouver(温哥华)to the sophisticated European flair of Montreal(蒙特利尔)and Quebec City(魁北克城). Canada's capital city is Ottawa(渥太华), Ontario, famous for its cultured yet friendly atmosphere. Often mistaken for the nation's capital, Toronto(多伦多)is probably the best known Canadian city, in large part due to the Toronto International Film Festival, the CN Tower(加拿大国家电视塔)and major sports franchises, including the Blue Jays(蓝鸟棒球队), the Toronto Maple Leafs(多伦多枫叶队)and the Raptors(猛龙队).

In addition to city destinations, a wide-ranging geography shapes exceptional natural beauty, wide open spaces, mountains and waterways, making this country ideal for many sports and outdoor adventures. Whether you are looking for nice hiking trails, golf courses or want to up the thrill(惊险)factor by heli-skiing or dog-sledding, Canada has a vacation for you.

Read the passage aloud and choose the best answer to complete each statement.

(1) Canada is one of the world's most ethnically diverse and multicultural nations, because _____.

    A. it has the population of approximately 35 million

    B. it is world's second largest country

    C. it shares the world's longest land border with the United States

    D. many people immigrate from other countries

(2) Toronto is one of the most popular city destinations, because _____.

    A. it is the best known Canadian city

B. it is the capital of Canada

C. it has sophisticated Latin flair

D. it has heli-skiing and dog-sledding in four seasons

(3) Based on the text, which of the following statements is NOT true?

A. Canada's common border with the United States is the world's longest land border.

B. Queen Elizabeth II is the head of state and has executive power in Canada.

C. As the second largest country in the world, Canada has a land mass that covers five time zones.

D. Canada has numerous French heritages, each offering its own Canadian urban experience.

(4) According to the last paragraph, Canada is also a good destination for _____.

A. shopping   B. physical training

C. immigration   D. education

 扫一扫，有答案。

Watch the short video twice, and complete the following requirements.

Step 1: Watch the video and take notes of what you have watched or heard. Compare the notes with your desk mate.

Step 2: Watch the video again and fill in the blanks in the following sentences with what you have watched or heard.

Summary:

1. In the world, there are unique places, rich in culture, _____ nature, and congenial to travelers.

2. Welcome to Canada! It is a culturally diverse nation with people of British and _____ origins.

3. Over one third of Canadians live in the country's three largest cities: Montreal, Toronto, and _____.

4. The Niagara Falls Ontario is one of the world's most _____ waterfalls and the Canadian Rocky is a vast and protected wildness area.

5. The Canadian Rocky is a vast and _____ wildness area with numbers recreational and scenic attractions.

 扫一扫，看视频。

Part Five Consolidation
第五部分：巩固练习

Practical Writing 应用文写作

Arrival Form /Entry Form
出入境表

In the flight from one country to another, the most important task for the tour leader is to ask the members of group to fill in the arrival or entry form. The form varies from country to country. When people enter into the United States, they need to complete arrival form, I-94 form. The form must be completed by all persons except U.S. citizens, returning resident aliens with immigrant visas, and Canadian Citizens visiting or in transit. Type or print legibly with pen in ALL CAPITAL LETTERS. All information should be filled in English. Do not write on the back of this form. This form is in two parts. They are Arrival Record (Item 1 through 13) and the Departure Record (Item 14 through 17). When all items are completed, present this form to the U.S. Immigration and Naturalization Service Inspector at arrival of the airport.

Suppose you are the tour leader who escorts a tour group to the United States for a holiday. Fill out the arrival card for the tour member who needs your help using the following outlines.

Arrival Card

Family Name 姓	Birth Date (Day/Mo/Yr) 生日(日/月/年)
First (Given) Name 名	Country of Citizenship 国籍
Sex (Male or Female) 性别(男性 Male 或女性 Female)	Passport Number 护照号码
Airline & Flight Number 航空公司及班机号码	Country Where You Live 居住国
City Where You Boarded 搭乘飞机城市	City Where Visa Was Issued 取得签证城市
Date Issued (Day/Mo/Yr) 取得签证日期(日/月/年)	Address While in the United State (Number and Street) 在美国的住址(门牌号及街名)
City and State 市名及州名	Departure Number 离境号码
Immigration and Naturalization Service 移民局	I-94 Departure Record I-94离境记录

Translation for the Tour Leader 领队翻译

1. Translate the following sentences into English with the words or phrases given.

(1)飞机已降落(land)在新加坡樟宜机场，现在是当地时间上午十一点，室外温度20摄氏度。

(2) 可以帮我调一下风量(airflow)吗？风正对着这位老人吹。
(3) 我们旅行团的一些成员不会说英语，请问你们有中文报纸或杂志吗？
(4) 这位女士因为晕机(airsickness)不舒服，可以给她把座位调到前排吗？
(5) 到英国我们是早一天(gain)还是晚一天(lose)？

 扫一扫，做翻译。

2. Translate the following sentences into Chinese with the words or phrases given.

(1) It is time for lunch. Please put down our tray tables (小桌板) and bring back our seats to the upright position.

(2) The plane is flying from Beijing to Seattle with a two-hour stopover (短暂停留) in Tokyo.

(3) We have just been informed by the captain (机长) that our departure will be delayed on account of big fog.

(4) Excuse me. We are passing through some turbulence (乱流) right now. Would you please fasten your seat belt?

(5) The call button and reading light is above your head. Press the call button to summon a flight attendant (乘务员).

 扫一扫，做翻译。

本章参考文献

[1] 曹银玲. 出境领队实务[M]. 北京：旅游教育出版社，2012.
[2] 王远梅. 空乘英语[M]. 北京：国防工业出版社，2010.
[3] 王健民. 出境旅游领队实务[M]. 5版. 北京：旅游教育出版社，2016.
[4] 黄恢月，仉向明. 出境旅游领队工作案例解析[M]. 北京：旅游教育出版社，2008.
[5] 袁智敏，仉向明. 领队英语[M]. 2版. 北京：旅游教育出版社，2008.
[6] 美国英语介绍.[EB/OL] 百度文库(2013).
http://wenku.baidu.com/view/61f21f9402d276a200292ed3.html
[7] http://www.learning-english-online.net/areas/cultural-studies/english-speaking-countries/canada/
[8] http://v.youku.com/v_show/id_XMTgxNTc4OTcxMg==.html

Chapter 4

抵达目的地
Arrival at Destination Countries

Learning Focus 学习要点

- **Case Study**
  The Police in Saipan Gets on the Coach
- **Listening Comprehension**
  Landing Announcement
- **Situational Dialogue**
  Task 4-1 Entry Formalities
  　　　—At the Entry Office
  Task 4-2 Luggage Reclaim
  　　　—Lost Baggage Report
  Task 4-3 Customs Inspection
  　　　—Customs Declaration
  Task 4-4 Contact with the Local Guide
  　　　—Meeting the Local Guide
- **ABC about Destination Countries**
  ABC about Brazil
- **Consolidation**
  Practical Writing: Customs Declaration
  Translation for Tour Leader

- ◆ 案例分析
  塞班的警察上了旅游车
- ◆ 听力训练
  飞机着陆通知
- ◆ 情景对话
  ①办理入境手续
  ——入境处
  ②提取行李
  ——报告行李遗失
  ③海关检查
  ——海关申报
  ④与地陪接洽
  ——与地陪见面
- ◆ 目的地国家概况
  巴西概况
- ◆ 巩固练习
  应用文写作：海关申报单
  领队翻译

出境领队英语

Part One Case Study
第一部分：案例分析

The Police in Saipan Gets on the Coach
塞班的警察上了旅游车

One tour group arrived at Saipan. While the tour leader was queuing for visa issues, a 9-year-old boy, one of the tour members, ran about in the hall. The boy's father asked his child not to run here and there, but the boy turned a deaf ear to his father, that made him angry. Then, the father rebuked his son, patted his son's forehead with his hand.

Out of the arrival hall, the tour leader met the local tour guide and the tour members began to get on the coach. Then, two policemen got on the coach and asked seriously, "Just now, who treated his own child rudely? Please go to the police station with us". The tour leader was quick-minded and said politely, "Can I say a few words about it?" The police nodded. The tour leader said, "We are from China. Chinese families usually have only one child. This father loves his son very much. What he did is just to stop his son from disturbing others in the hall." The police said, "Please tell the father that he should do an apology to his son." And then, the two policemen got down the coach and left.

 扫一扫，看译文。

1. Study the case carefully. Decide whether the following statements are true or false and write T for true and F for false.

(1) _____ The tour leader should take care of the child because he is one member of the tour group.

(2) _____ The father should take care of the child because he is the legal guardian of the child.

(3) _____ The local guide should take care of the child because the tour leader is busy with visa issues.

(4) _____ It is funny that a father does an apology to his child. And a father can do whatever he likes to care for his child.

(5) _____ The tour leader should refuse the policemen to get on the coach and protect the legal right of the tour members.

 扫一扫，有答案。

Chapter 4
抵达目的地
Arrival at Destination Countries

2. Divide the class into several groups for a brief discussion. One student makes a presentation of the main points discussed and the others give comments on the presentation.

Discussions: What should the tour leader do to reduce misunderstanding between tour members and local people?

Comments:

(1)_____

(2)_____

(3)_____

(4)_____

(5)_____

 小知识

抵达目的地领队的工作

从航班降落目的地机场的那一刻,你所乘坐航班的舱门开启时,领队的工作就开始啦!

1. 客人再召集。旅行团的飞机座位一般在飞机尾部,且分布零散,客人之间彼此不熟悉,因此航班抵达后又必须重新召集客人,一方面派发入境资料,一方面讲解入境流程。召集的地点一般在有明显标志、旅客较少的安静处。
2. 移民过关。领队带领游客按照程序办理相关入境手续。通常称为"过三关",即:卫生检疫、证照查验、海关检查。
3. 领取托运行李。领队带领游客到航空公司的托运行李领取处领取自己的行李。如发生行李延误、破损、丢失等情况,应协助游客到机场查询处申报,交由航空公司处理。
4. 兑换货币。当地货币一般在抵达机场后有机构(银行或政府授权兑换点)兑换,领队应引导前往,但不要过多介入兑换过程,一般只告诉兑换地点,自己不参与客人的兑换活动。
5. 接洽地陪。带领游客到达入口,与前来迎接的当地导游会合。会合后领队应主动与导游交换名片,并对其通信方式进行确认,进行简单的行程交流。

Part Two Listening Comprehension
第二部分:听力训练

Words and Expressions

Auckland	n.	奥克兰	detach	v.	分离;派遣
Celsius	n.	摄氏度	disembark	v.	登陆;下车
Fahrenheit	n.	华氏度	retrieve	v.	取回
taxi	v.	滑行	procedure	n.	程序;步骤

47

Landing Announcement 飞机着陆通知

1. Listen to the passage and fill in the blanks with the missing information.

 扫一扫，听一听。

Our plane has (1)_____ at Auckland airport. The local time is 13:00 p.m. The temperature outside is 13 degrees Celsius, ((2)_____ degrees Fahrenheit.) The plane is (3)_____. For your safety, please stay (4)_____ for the time being. When the aircraft stops completely and the Fasten Seat Belt sign is (5)_____. Please detach the (6)_____, take all your carry-on items and disembark (please detach the seat belt and take all your carry-on items and passport to complete the (7)_____ in the terminal). Please be cautious when retrieving items from the (8)_____. Your checked baggage may be claimed in the baggage claim area. The transit passengers please go to the (9)_____ in the waiting hall to complete the procedures. Welcome to Auckland, wish you a pleasant day. Thank you! Thank you for selecting (10)_____ for your travel today and we look forward to serving you again.

扫一扫，有答案。

2. Fill in the blanks with the words and expressions given below. Change their forms when necessary.

retrieve	safety	carry-on	detach	disembark
cautious	land	degree	taxi	formality

Good afternoon, Ladies and Gentlemen:

Our plane will be (1)_____ at Auckland airport in 10 minutes. The ground temperature is 10 (2)_____ Celsius. The plane will be (3)_____ down the runway soon. Please be seated and not (4)_____ your seat belt. Seat backs and tables should be (5)_____ to the upright position. All personal computers and electronic devices should be turned off before you (6)_____. And please be (7)_____ enough and make sure that your (8)_____ items, passports and entry (9)_____ are securely stowed. For your

(10)_____, we will be dimming the cabin lights for landing. Thank you!

  扫一扫，有答案。

Part Three Situational Dialogue
第三部分：情景对话

Task 4-1 Entry Formalities 办理入境手续

At the Entry Office 入境处

1. Listen to the dialogue carefully and fill in the table with correct information.

  扫一扫，听一听。

The formalities to show	The duration of the trip	The hotel to stay	The purpose of the trip

  扫一扫，有答案。

2. Listen again, and do a situational dialogue with your partner.

Task 4-2 Luggage Reclaim 提取行李

Lost Baggage Report 报告行李遗失

1. Listen to the dialogue and choose the best answer according to the dialogue.

  扫一扫，听一听。

49

(1) Which picture shows the lost baggage?

A.

B.

C.

(2) If the baggage is found, it will be sent to _____.
   A. airport   B. hotel   C. Baggage Claim

 扫一扫，有答案。

2. Suppose you were a tour leader and your deskmate is the tourist who lost her luggage. Do the situational dialogue again with following key words or expressions.

(1) What can I do for you...?
(2) How many pieces of baggage...?
(3) Can you... ?
(4) ...a gray medium-sized Samsonite...
(5) Would you mind...
(6) Please deliver to...
(7) Sure, ...
(8) It's my pleasure...

Task 4-3 Customs Inspection 海关检查

Customs Declaration 海关申报

1. Listen to the dialogue carefully and fill in the blanks with correct information.

 扫一扫，听一听。

A (1)_____ went to the United States for (2)_____. At the customs, he showed his (3)_____ and (4)_____ to the customs officer. Not bringing in any (5)_____ but some (6)_____ for (7)____, he had nothing to (8)_____. Finally, the officer returned his forms and asked him to (9)_____ and take them back when he (10)_____ the States.

Chapter 4

抵达目的地
Arrival at Destination Countries

 扫一扫,有答案。

2. Listen to a passage and retell what you've heard with given key words or expressions below.

 扫一扫,听一听。

(1) U.S. Residents — Declare...
(2) Visitors(Non-Residents)— Declare...
Declare...
(3) Duty — CBP officers ...
U.S. Residents are normally entitled to ...
Visitors (non-residents) ...
Duty ...

 扫一扫,有答案。

Task 4-4 Contact with the Local Guide 与地陪接洽

Meeting the Local Guide 与地陪见面

1. Listen to the dialogue and fill in the blanks with the missing information.

 扫一扫,听一听。

 (L=Local Guide; T=Tour Leader)
L: Good afternoon. Welcome to the U.S. (1)_____.
T: Me too. (2)_____.
L: It's my pleasure. (3)_____?
T: Great. (4)_____.
L: That's fine. (5)_____?
T: Yes, (6)_____. All the guests are here.
L: OK. Let's go.

51

扫一扫，有答案。

2. Listen to the dialogue again, and complete following dialogues by translating the Chinese into English orally.

(L=Local Guide;　T=Tour Leader)

L: Good afternoon. (1)_____.(欢迎您到加拿大。)
T: Thanks for your coming. (2)_____(很高兴您能来接我们。)
L: It's my pleasure. (3)_____(旅途愉快吗？)
T: Great. (4)_____(旅途一切顺利！)
L: That's fine. (5)_____(现在我能带您去酒店吗？)
T: Yes, that would be great. (6)_____(所有的客人都在这。)
L: OK. Let's go.

扫一扫，有答案。

Part Four ABC about Destination Countries
第四部分：目的地国家概况

Brazil 巴西

One of the world's most captivating places, Brazil is South America's giant, a dazzling country of powdery white-sand beaches, pristine rain forests and wild, rhythm-filled metropolises(大都市). Brazil's attractions extend from enchanting, frozen-in-time colonial towns to dramatic landscapes of red-rock canyons(峡谷), thundering waterfalls and idyllic tropical islands. Add to that, Brazil's biodiversity(生物多样性)boasts the greatest collection of plant and animal species found anywhere on earth.

Brazil offers a lot of striking attractions that combines all types of tourism starting by ecotourism and city tour for it is full of incredible(难以置信的)and various landscapes ranging from striking beaches to diverse rainforest. There's horseback riding in the swamps, kayaking in the flooded forests, whale-watching(观鲸)off the coast, surfing off palm-fringed beaches and snorkeling(潜泳)in the crystal-clear rivers-all part of the great Brazilian experience.

No less entrancing is the prospect of doing nothing, aside from sinking into warm sands and soaking up a glorious stretch of beach. Brazil's most famous celebration, Carnival(狂欢

Chapter 4
抵达目的地
Arrival at Destination Countries

节)storms though the country's cities and towns with hip-shaking samba(桑巴舞), dazzling costumes and carefree joie de vivre (生活乐趣). Wherever there's music, the carefree lust for life tends to appear-whether dancing with Carioca(卡里奥克舞) at samba clubs or following powerful drumbeats through the streets.

　　With so much going for them, it's no wonder that Brazilians say "Deus e Brasileiro" ("God is Brazilian"). How else to explain the treasure of natural and cultural riches all across this amazing country?

Read the passage aloud and choose the best answer to complete each statement.

1. In the first paragraph, "captivating" means _____.
   A. attractive　　　B. relaxing　　　C. peaceful　　　D. picturesque

2. Brazil offers big adventures for travelers except _____?
   A. horse-riding　　B. whale-watching　C. snorkeling　　D. Scuba diving

3. _____ is the most famous celebration in Brazil.
   A. Carnival　　　B. Christmas Day　　C. New Year　　D. Passover

4. In the last paragraph, "God is Brazilian" means _____.
   A. God loves Brazilians more
   B. Brazilians are the descendants of God
   C. the land of Brazil is given by God
   D. Brazil is endowed with profound natural and cultural resources

 扫一扫，有答案。

Watch the short video twice, and complete the following requirements.

Step 1: Watch the video and take notes of what you have watched or heard. Compare the notes with your desk mate.

Step 2: Watch the video again and fill in the blanks in the following sentences with what you have watched or heard.

Summary:

1. Brazil is located in South America and the main language spoken in Brazil is _____.

2. Rio De Janeiro is famous for its celebration and for _____ the 2016 Summer Olympic Games.

3. Coffee is a product from Brazil that is sold to many other _____. Brazil Nuts are also tasty, and many people want to enjoy them.

4. Amazon Rainforest is the _____ in the world. With many trees and animals, this forest is very special and needs to be protected.

5. Brazil drumming and musical culture is well-known throughout South America. The most famous festival in Brazil is _____.

扫一扫，看视频。

Part Five Consolidation
第五部分：巩固练习

Practical Writing 应用文写作

Customs Declaration
海关申报单

Before the entry of the destination country, officers at customs will check the baggage of the tourists to find out whether there is any object illegal or necessary to pay duties. Anyone who fails to pass the check will be denied to enter. This form must be completed by all persons who need to declare their belongings. Type or print legibly with pen in ALL CAPITAL LETTERS. All information should be filled in English. When all items are completed, present this form to customs at the airport.

Suppose you are the tourists, fill out the customs declaration. Don't hesitate to ask the tour leader if you have any problems when you fill in the form.

Customs Declaration

Each arriving traveler or head of family must provide the following information (only ONE written declaration per family is required):

每一位入境美国的游客或一家之主必须提供以下资料 (一个家庭只需申报一份)：

Chapter 4

抵达目的地
Arrival at Destination Countries

1. Family Name: Last_____
   First(Given) _____ Middle Initial_____
   (姓名：姓_____ 名_____ 中间名_____)

2. Birth date：Day_____ Month_____ Year_____
   (出生日期：日_____ 月_____ 年_____)

3. Number of family members traveling with you (与你同行的家庭成员人数):

4. a. U.S. street address (hotel name/destination)：[在美居住地址(旅馆名称/目的地)]:
   b. City (城市)_____ c. State (州)_____

5. Passport issued by (country)：(发照国家)

6. Passport number：(护照号码)

7. Country of Residence：(居住国家)

8. Countries visited on this trip prior to U.S. arrival：_____
   (此次旅游时来美国之前去过的国家)

9. Airline/Flight No. or Vessel Name: _____
   (航空公司/班机号码或船名)：

10. The purpose of my trip is or was BUSINESS   ○ YES ○ NO
    (此次旅程的目的主要是商务)   ○ 是 ○ 否

11. I am (We are) bringing：
    [我(我们)携带]：
    a. fruits, plants, food, or insects?   ○ YES ○ NO
       (水果、植物、食物或昆虫？)   ○ 是 ○ 否
    b. meats, animals, or animal/wildlife products?   ○ YES ○ NO
       (肉类、动物或动物/野生动物制品？)   ○ 是 ○ 否
    c. disease agents, cell cultures, or snails?   ○ YES ○ NO
       (带病原体、细胞培养或蜗牛？)   ○ 是 ○ 否
    d. soil or have you visited a farm/ranch/pasture outside   ○ YES ○ NO
       the United States?
    (土壤或你曾经去过美国境外的农场或牧场吗？)   ○ 是 ○ 否

12. I have (We have) been in close proximity of   ○ YES ○ NO
    (such as touching or handling) livestock outside the United States?：
    [我有(我们有)靠近(如触碰或接触)牲畜？]   ○ 是 ○ 否

13. I am (we are) carrying currency or monetary instruments over   ○ YES ○ NO
    10,000 U.S. or the foreign equivalent.
    (你携带现金或财物，其价值超过一万美金
    或相当于一万美金的外币吗？)   ○ 是 ○ 否

55

14. I have (We have) commercial merchandise: (article for sale, samples used for soliciting orders, or goods that are not considered personal effects) [我(我们)有携带商品：(贩卖物品、商业样品或任何不属于个人所有的物品)]	○ YES ○NO ○是 ○否
15. Residents-the total value of all good, including commercial merchandise I/We have purchased or acquired abroad, (including gifts for someone else, but not items mailed to the U.S.) and am/are bringing to the U.S. is: (美国居民: 我们带入美国所有物品(包含商品及礼品，但不包含邮寄入美国的物品)的总价值为)： _____	
16. Visitors – the total value of all article that will remain in the U.S., including commercial merchandise is: (观光客——将留在美国境内的物品价值为(包含商品))： _____	
Read the instruction on the back of this form. Space is provided to list all the items you must declare. (请阅读本表背面的说明，请将须申报的物品在空格内列出) I HAVE READ THE IMPORTANT INFORMATION ON THE REVERSE SIDE OF THIS FORM AND HAVE MADE A TRUTHFUL DECLARATION. (我已阅读过背面的说明，且已如实申报) Signature; Date (day/month/year) 签名及日期(日/月/年)_____	

Translation for the Tour Leader 领队翻译

1. Translate the following sentences into English with the words or phrases given.

(1) 请让您的乘客将他们的入境卡(arrival card)放在护照(passport)中，按照名单上的顺序，依次通过。

(2) 我们将把入境登记表(entry card)和海关申报表(custom declaration)发给乘客填写。

(3) 我是旅行团的领队，我们持有团体旅游签证。能让我最后一个通过吗？

(4) 对不起，先生。我的旅行箱的把手坏了。我应该到哪里去申报破损？

(5) 这是您的护照，您可以到行李提取处提取您的行李，然后进行海关检查。海关官员(customs officer)检查后，会在您的表上盖上章(stamp)。

 扫一扫，做翻译。

2. Translate the following sentences into Chinese with the words or phrases given.

(1) If the airline should lose your baggage, report the loss to the airline agent (航空公司代理). The agent will be responsible for your loss.

(2) You are not allowed to bring the fruits into the United States. I have to confiscate (没收) these.

(3) Whenever TYPE or PRINT is mentioned, it means write in capital letters. You have to fill in two forms, namely I-94 Arrival-Departure Record (入境离境卡) and Customs form.

(4) I'm from the Quarantine Authority (卫生防疫部门). May I have your Health Certificate and Vaccination Certificate (防疫证明)?

(5) If you are coming on visitor visa and your visa is expiring next month, immigration officer grants (授权) you six months stay, and then you can stay here for six month.

 扫一扫，做翻译。

本章参考文献

[1]曹银玲. 出境领队实务[M]. 北京：旅游教育出版社，2012.

[2]王远梅. 空乘英语[M]. 北京：国防工业出版社，2010.

[3]王健民. 出境旅游领队实务[M]. 5版. 北京：旅游教育出版社，2016.

[4]黄恢月，仉向明. 出境旅游领队工作案例解析[M]. 北京：旅游教育出版社，2008.

[5]袁智敏，仉向明. 领队英语[M]. 2版. 北京：旅游教育出版社，2008.

[6]http://v.youku.com/v_show/id_XMjEwNjM3ODgwNA==.html

Chapter 5

联系地陪
Contact with Local Guides

Learning Focus 学习要点

- ◆ **Case Study**
  Cancellation of Tourist Sites
- ◆ **Listening Comprehension**
  Adjustment of the Itinerary
- ◆ **Situational Dialogue**
  Task 5-1 Contact the Local Guide at the Airport
  　　　　　—Handing Over the Luggage
  　　　　　—On the Way to the Hotel
  Task 5-2 Discuss the Travel Schedule
  　　　　　—Discussing the Itinerary
  Task 5-3 Handling Complaints
  　　　　　—Disputes Over the Room Standard
  Task 5-4 At the Restaurant
  　　　　　—Meal Problem
- ◆ **ABC about Destination Countries**
  ABC about Russia
- ◆ **Consolidation**
  Practical Writing: A Letter of Complaint
  Translation for Tour Leader

- ◆ 案例分析
  取消旅游景点
- ◆ 听力训练
  调整线路
- ◆ 情景对话
  ①在机场与地陪接洽
  　——交接行李
  　——前往酒店途中
  ②商谈旅游行程
  　——讨论线路
  ③投诉处理
  　——住宿标准纠纷
  ④餐厅就餐
  　——饭菜问题
- ◆ 目的地国家概况
  俄罗斯概况
- ◆ 巩固练习
  应用文写作：投诉信
  领队翻译

Part One Case Study
第一部分：案例分析

Cancellation of Tourist Sites
取消旅游景点

Ms. Xu and her five family members joined a Southeast Asia tour launched by an international travel service. According to the contract, the travel service was to offer a night visit. When the group arrived at the destination, some tourists proposed to cancel the night visit because it was raining; in addition, all of them felt very tired after a long journey. With the permission from most of the tourists, the local guide cancelled the night visit. However, Ms. Xu and her family insisted the program. The tour leader refused the Xu's request He claimed that his travel service could only satisfy the needs of the most guests, and most of them had agreed to cancel the night visit. Back in China, Ms. Xu immediately complained to the local tourism administration and asked the travel service for compensation.

 扫一扫，看译文。

1. Study the case carefully. Decide whether the following statements are true or false and write T for true and F for false.

(1) _____ The tourist sites in the travel schedule can be cancelled subject to the approval of most tourists.

(2) _____ The night visit was cancelled because of the force majeure.

(3) _____ The local guide has the right to cancel tourist attractions with permission of the tour leader.

(4) _____ The tour leader has the right to cancel the attractions with permission of the domestic travel service.

(5) _____ The tour leader is not to be blamed because he just implemented the principle of the minority obeying the majority.

 扫一扫，有答案。

2. Divide the class into several groups for a brief discussion. One student makes a presentation of the main points discussion and the others give comments on the presentation.

Discussions: What should a tour leader do when tourists proposed to cancel the sites specified in the travel schedule?

Comments:

(1)_____

(2)_____

(3)_____

(4)_____

(5)_____

 扫一扫，有答案。

 小知识 ─────────────────────────────

领队联系地陪

1. 旅游团抵达后，地陪会站在明显的地方举起站牌，领队应主动前往联系地陪。
2. 领队应及时与地陪接洽，告之组团社的名称、客源地，并自我介绍。
3. 与地陪核实旅行团实到人数，集中清点行李，集合登车。
4. 与地陪核实行程计划。如果地陪的行程有出入，领队应请示组团社批准。
5. 离开机场赴酒店途中，地陪介绍下榻酒店，宣布当日或次日的安排活动以及集合时间、地点，领队应予协助。

Part Two Listening Comprehension
第二部分：听力训练

Words and Expressions

respond	v.	做出反应	specify	v.	指定；详细说明
evaluate	v.	评价；评估	proposal	n.	提议
feasible	adj.	可行的	appropriate	adj.	恰当的；合适的

Adjustment of the Itinerary 调整线路

1. Listen to the passage and fill in the blanks with the missing information you have heard.

 扫一扫，听一听。

A tour leader should respond to tourists if they want to (1) _____. Usually a tour leader should adhere to the itinerary that is specified (2) _____. He should not change the itinerary or the travel schedule (3) _____. If tourists want to change the itinerary, the tour leader should (4) _____. Provided that their proposal is feasible, he may make (5) _____. Appropriate adjustment of the itinerary should be made in accordance with the (6)_____. In addition, the adjustment of the itinerary cannot be made unless the tour leader acquires the approval of both the local travel service and (7)_____. The tour leader should inform tourists of the change and try to get (8) _____.

扫一扫，有答案。

2. Fill in the blanks with the words and expressions given below and change their forms when necessary.

evaluation	adjust	respond	application	specify	feasibility

(1) The tour leader should _____ to tourists if they want to change the itinerary.

(2) Itinerary _____ in the contract should not be changed at will.

(3) The tour leader should _____ the tourists' suggestion about the change of the itinerary.

(4) If the suggestions are _____, the tour leader may adjust the itinerary subject to approval of the travel service.

(5) Any _____ of the itinerary should be made in accordance with the travel schedule.

(6) The majority rule cannot be _____ for change of the itinerary or travel schedule.

 扫一扫，有答案。

Chapter 5
联系地陪
Contact with Local Guides

Part Three Situational Dialogue
第三部分：情景对话

Words and Expressions

cart	n.	运货车	Travel Agency		旅行社
safety precaution		安全预防	inn	n.	旅馆
rank	v.	排列	access	n.	(使用的)机会
pull up to	v.	停下	lobby	n.	大厅
St. Paul's Cathedral		圣保罗大教堂	Buckingham Palace		白金汉宫
principal	adj.	最重要的	package tour	n.	跟团旅游
complain	v.	投诉	a hard nut to crack		难事

Task 5-1 Contact the Local Guide at the Airport 在机场与地陪接洽

Handing Over the Luggage 交接行李

1. Listen to the dialogue and write numbers in the blanks to show the correct order of the conversation.

扫一扫，听一听。

(T=Tour Leader; L=Local Guide)

____ (1) **L:** OK. Attention, everybody. Now, follow me please. We're moving to the coach.

____ (2) **L:** I see. Let's check them together and hand it over to the luggage man.

____ (3) **L:** Is everybody here now? Our bus is outside the airport.

____ (4) **L:** Ms. Chen, how many pieces of luggage do you have in all?

____ (5) **T:** Oh, let me check. Yes, everybody is here.

____ (6) **T:** All right. (*To the group members*) Ladies and gentlemen, attention, please. Please put your luggage on these carts. The local guide and I will take care of it.

____ (7) **T:** There are 22 pieces altogether.

扫一扫，有答案。

2. Listen to the dialogue again, and act it out with your deskmate. Pay attention to your body language.

63

On the Way to the Hotel 前往酒店途中

1. Listen to dialogue carefully and complete the following sentences with what you have heard.

 扫一扫，听一听。

(1) Teresa is the local guide from _____.
(2) It will take _____ from the airport to the hotel.
(3) Tourists should remain seated on the coach and do not stretch your heads or _____ _____.
(4) The tour group will head for _____ after they load the luggage.
(5) Hotel offers access to internet as well as _____ within the United States.
(6) Jane will be meeting us at the entrance of the hotel to _____.
(7) The local guide will meet tourists again in the lobby _____.

 扫一扫，有答案。

2. Role play: Suppose you are a tour leader and your deskmate is a local guide. Make a dialogue on the way to the hotel using following tips.

➢ go to the hotel;
➢ remain in your seat;
➢ not stretch your heads or hands out of the window;
➢ check your luggage;
➢ make sure you have taken your bags with you before leaving the coach;
➢ hope you have a wonderful vacation.

Task 5-2 Discuss the Travel Schedule 商谈旅游行程

Discussing the Itinerary 讨论线路

1. Listen to the dialogue and answer the following questions.

扫一扫，听一听。

64

Chapter 5
联系地陪
Contact with Local Guides

(1) What are they talking about?

　　A. itinerary　　　　　　　　B. time　　　　　　　　C. weather

(2) How long will they stay in London?

　　A. one day　　　　　　　　B. two days　　　　　　C. three days

(3) Which site is the must-see attraction in London?

　　A. St. Paul's Cathedral　　　B. Tower of London　　C. Buckingham Palace

(4) Where do they have their lunch?

　　A. in the hotel　　　　　　　B. at the restaurant　　C. on the travel boat

　　扫一扫，有答案。

2. Listen to the dialogue again and choose the most professional statement that matches meanings of the italicized parts from the following choices.

　　(T=Tour Leader; L=Local Guide)

Episode 1

T: It seems everything is all right. ***Let's start discussing the itinerary.***

A. Will you start discussing the itinerary?

B. It's better to start discussing the itinerary now.

C. Shall we start discussing the itinerary?

Episode 2

L: OK, Mr. Chen. ***Do you think where you would visit?***

A. Do you think where you would like to visit?

B. Have you got anything in mind that you would like to visit?

C. Have you thought where you want to visit?

Episode 3

T: The time is far from enough, but ***we want to visit a city like London which has many world well-known places of interest.***

A. Can we visit a city like London which has many world well-known places of interest?

B. Is it possible for us to visit a city like London which has many world well-known places of interest?

C. Shall we visit a city like London which has many world well-known places of interest?

Episode 4

L: Don't worry. *I am sure I will let you see as many places as possible.*

A. I promise I'll let you see as many places as possible.

B. Take it easy. I will try my best to take you to many places you can see.

C. Anyhow it is not the end of the world. I'll try to let you see as many places as possible.

Episode 5

T: *Thank you. You are very considerate.*

A. Thank you. You are welcome.

B. Thank you. You are good.

C. Thank you. It's really very thoughtful of you.

 扫一扫，有答案。

Task 5-3 Handling Complaints 投诉处理

Disputes Over the Room Standard 住宿标准纠纷

1. Listen to the dialogue and choose the best answer according to information you've heard.

 扫一扫，听一听。

(1) Who is the receptionist?
   A. Pan Xiaoyun.   B. Simon.
   C. Zhao Jiming.   D. Jack.

(2) What is wrong with the guest?
   A. He is complaining about food.   B. He wants room service.
   C. He is not happy with the room. D. He is checking out.

(3) What is the solution?
   A. He has moved to another room.

B. Nothing has been done.

C. He left the hotel.

D. The receptionist would send a house maid to fresh the air and make the bed again.

 扫一扫，有答案。

2. **Listen to the dialogue again and rearrange the order of pictures based on the sequence of events in the conversation. Describe the pictures according to the right order.**

 扫一扫，有答案。

Task 5-4 At the Restaurant 餐厅就餐

Meal Problem 饭菜问题

1. **Listen to the dialogue carefully and decide whether the following statements are true or false and write T for true and F for false.**

 扫一扫，听一听。

(1) The group members complained about the quality of the meals.

(2) The group members had meals in the Western restaurant.

(3) The tour leader was willing to make the payment for the additional dishes.

(4) The local guide refused to talk with the manager.

 扫一扫，有答案。

2. **Listen to the dialogue again, and act it out with your deskmate.**

Part Four ABC about Destination Countries
第四部分：目的地国家概况

Russia 俄罗斯

Russia, also officially the Russian Federation is a country in Eurasia. At 17,075,200 square kilometers, it is the largest country in the world by surface area, covering more than one-eighth of the Earth's inhabited(可居住的) land area, and the ninth most populous, with over 144 million people at the end of March 2016.

Russian culture and art is extremely brilliant and colorful. This piece of land breeds so many famous figures such as Pushkin (普希金), Tolstoy (托尔斯泰) and all literary giants create a number of great art masterpieces. Perhaps only when we stepped into the land of Russia can we really understand how it feels like in Russia.

Russia is rich in tourism resources. Moscow's Red Square (莫斯科红场), the magnificent Kremlin (克里姆林宫) and other attractions have been world-famous for centuries. St. Petersburg (圣彼得堡), the second largest city is an elegant and romantic city. Quiet and wide Neva (涅瓦河) and criss-crossing ancient canal constitute the city's water network system. In Russia you can also see the world's deepest and most pure lake, Baikal (贝加尔湖), or take train going through the lush Siberian forest (西伯利亚森林), to see the beautiful scenery of the Black Sea (黑海). You can have a cultural tour, go to Mariinsky Theater (马林斯基剧院) to see a ballet show, or go to The TRETYAKOV GALLERY (特列季亚科夫美术馆) to see those who handed down the masterpiece. Of course, you can not miss the Winter Palace where there are more than 200 years collections that will be a feast for your eyes.

Rich cultural heritage and great natural variety place Russia among the most popular tourist destinations in the world. The country contains 23 UNESCO (联合国教科文组织) World Heritage Sites, while many more are on UNESCO's tentative lists. Taking up an immense space, a home to different nationalities and cultures, it's often called a bridge between the East and the West. You can spend a lifetime exploring it without ever unveiling all its mysteries or feel at home over a week-end.

Read the passage aloud and choose the best answer to complete each statement.

1. Russia is the largest country in the world by surface area, covering more than _____ of the world's inhabited land area.

    A. one-sixth   B. one-eighth
    C. one-seventh   D. one-ninth

2. St. Petersburg is the second largest city in Russia which presents tourists an _____ look.

   A. old and shabby   B. elegant and romantic
   C. old and solemn   D. exquisite and beautiful

3. Tourists can have a cultural tour and enjoy more than 200 years collections in _____.

   A. Winter Palace   B. Summer Palace
   C. Mariinsky Theater   D. Moscow's Red Square

4. Based on the text, which of the following statements is NOT true?

   A. Russia is often called a bridge between the East and the West.
   B. In Russia tourist can see the world's deepest and most pure lake, Baikal.
   C. There are 23 World Heritage Sites in Russia and no more will be inscribed by UNESCO.
   D. the Russian Federation is both an Asian country and a European country.

扫一扫，有答案。

Watch the short video twice, and complete the following requirements.

Step 1: Watch the video and take notes of what you have watched or heard. Compare the notes with your desk mate.

Step 2: Watch the video again and fill in the blanks in the following sentences with what you have watched or heard.

   Summary:

   1. Here stands the Kremlin located beyond the Red Wall; various _____ date back to the 15th century.

   2. Red Square is probably the most famous square in the world, but the name "red" doesn't refer to blood. in Russian it means _____.

   3. Uspensky Sobor is a successful combination of old Russian architecture and Italian renaissance, shining white and has five golden _____.

   4. The huge tsar cannon at the entrance to the Cathedral Square was never _____, but it became famous due to its mention in Tolstoy's novel War And Peace.

   5. It is a city within a city, the embodiment of the former power that stretches over the _____ country on earth.

 扫一扫，看视频。

Part Five Consolidation
第五部分：巩固练习

Practical Writing 应用文写作

A Letter of Complaint 投诉信

The process of travel consists of many different components and interrelated parts such as transportation, accommodation, attractions, activities, etc. As soon as guests arrive at a hotel, all the related departments of a hotel need to work together to provide them with proper goods and services. If guests are not content with the services offered by the hotel, they will certainly complain.

Generally, complaints can be expressed in two different ways, by telephone, or by letter. A complaint may be sent directly to the related departments or to the General Manager. After receiving the complaints, the hotel should look into the matter; then take appropriate measures to handle the complaints.

Suppose you are the General Manager of Crown Plaza Hotel, reply to Jane Clinton, the guest who has written a letter of complaint for receiving poor service during her stay at your hotel.

Outline:

(1) Your apologies and sympathies.

(2) Measures you will take.

(3) Compensation you will make.

(4) Your wish to offer better service.

Crown Plaza Hotel
No. 17, 4th Block, 1st Ring Road,
Hangzhou, Zhejiang

Attn: Mr. Lin Yunzhi
Dear Mr. Lin,

    As one of your regular guests, I'm writing to complain about my stay in your hotel. To be frank, I am terribly disappointed at your service as well as your hotel facilities. Firstly, when I checked in, your receptionists chatted aloud. I waited for almost twenty minutes before my luggage was sent up to my room. Moreover, the tap was out of order when I took a shower. Worst of all, the hotel failed to provide me with room service next morning. I find it unacceptable that you sold me a room, which was not similar to the description on your website, and therefore I claim a refund of RMB800. I sincerely hope that you could look into this matter and the problems mentioned above can be solved at your earliest convenience.

Yours sincerely,
Jane Clinton

Chapter 5

联系地陪
Contact with Local Guides

Translation for the Tour Leader 领队翻译

1. Translate the following sentences into English with the words or phrases given.

(1) 我觉得领队一点不负责(irresponsible)，带我们去了不干净的地方用餐，有好几位游客吃了东西都觉得难受(feel ill)。

(2) 我向地陪询问丢失行李事宜，他竟然很不配合(cooperate)，非常不友好，不愿意(was unwilling to)帮我向机场查询(inquire)。

(3) 我们对你们领队提供的服务很不满意，他对我们不管不问 (pay little attention)，不解决问题，老是带我们购物。

(4) 大家经过长途旅行后都希望好好休息，所以游客们提出取消(cancel)晚上的夜游(night visit)。

(5) 我的客人都又累又饿，附近有快餐店(fast-food restaurant) 没有？不如我们就近吃午餐，并休息(refreshment)一下。

扫一扫，做翻译。

2. Translate the following sentences into Chinese with the words or phrases given.

(1) We have made reservation for you at the hotel. Your luggage will be delivered (递送) to your room in the hotel.

(2) May I help you with your suitcase (手提箱)? How many pieces of baggage do you have altogether?

(3) Please pick up all your personal belongings and follow me to the Ground Transportation Center (地面运输中心).

(4) I'm terribly sorry for the day, but on our way to the airport, we got stuck in (陷入) the traffic jam. I really apologize (抱歉) for being late to meet you.

(5) Vienna enjoys high reputation for its historical and cultural sites (历史文化古迹). So, it might be a good idea to arrange one more tourist attraction each day and leave the last day for shopping and relaxation.

扫一扫，做翻译。

本章参考文献

[1]曹银玲. 出境领队实务[M]. 北京：旅游教育出版社，2012.

[2]赵冉冉. 导游应急处理一本通[M].北京：旅游教育出版社，2008.

[3]王健民. 出境旅游领队实务[M]. 5版. 北京：旅游教育出版社，2016.

[4]黄恢月，仇向明. 出境旅游领队工作案例解析[M]. 北京：旅游教育出版社，2008.

[5]袁智敏，仇向明. 领队英语[M]. 2版. 北京：旅游教育出版社，2008.

[6] http://www.zglxw.com/news/eluosi_14387.html

[7] http://www.iqiyi.com/w_19rto94yip.html

Chapter 6

下榻酒店
Hotel Check-in

Learning Focus 学习要点

◆ **Case Study**
　Breakfast Is Over!

◆ **Listening Comprehension**
　Service after Check-in

◆ **Situational Dialogue**
　Task 6-1　Checking in
　　　　　　—Bell Service
　Task 6-2　Concierge
　　　　　　—Keeping Valuables
　Task 6-3　Inquires in the Hotel
　　　　　　—Inquires about City Tour
　Task 6-4　Laundry Service
　　　　　　—Inquires about Laundry Service

◆ **ABC about Destination Countries**
　ABC about New Zealand

◆ **Consolidation**
　Practical Writing: Hotel Registration Card
　Translation for Tour Leader

◆ 案例分析
　早餐结束了!

◆ 听力训练
　入住酒店后的服务

◆ 情景对话
　①入住酒店
　　——行李交接服务
　②礼宾服务
　　——保管贵重物品
　③店内问询
　　——询问市内观光旅游
　④洗衣服务
　　——询问洗衣服务

◆ 目的地国家概况
　新西兰概况

◆ 巩固练习
　应用文写作: 酒店入住登记卡
　领队翻译

Part One Case Study
第一部分：案例分析

Breakfast Is Over!
早餐结束了！

A group of Chinese tourists arrived at Vienna, the capital of Austria. Most of them were the entrepreneurs of the destination town. After checked-in, the tour leader briefly introduced the customs, taboos and table manners of the destination country, but they were impatient and even felt disgusted, saying, "We Chinese should stand tall and not afraid of anything when we are abroad." Then, they hurried up to the own rooms.

Next morning, they went to the second floor to have Home Town buffet for their breakfast. The hotel restaurant provided various kinds of desserts, cheeses, jams and fresh fruits. Mr. Wu took a full plate of food without much consideration, but he just smelled it, leaving the food on the table. Then, he opened a dozen boxes of jams and cheeses without eating any. At this, the head of the restaurant, an old Austrian around 50 years old, came over and speaking to him baldly in blunt English: "In the past, Chinese people were poor and many Chinese didn't have enough food and even died of hunger. Now China is strong. Chinese people are rich, but it is so shameful that you wasted so much! Just go! Breakfast is over!"

 扫一扫，看译文。

1. Study the case carefully. Decide whether the following statements are true or false and write T for true and F for false.

(1) _____ The tour leader should introduce the custom, etiquette and relevant laws and regulations of the destination countries to the visitors.

(2) _____ Chinese should stand tall and not afraid of anything when they travel abroad.

(3) _____ Tourists have the right to eat or just leave the food on the table because they have paid for it.

(4) _____ The head of the restaurant rebuked the Chinese tourists because he thought the Chinese were rich.

 扫一扫，有答案。

Chapter 6
下榻酒店
Hotel Check-in

2. Divide the class into several groups for a brief discussion. One student makes a presentation of the main points of the case and the others give comments on it.

Discussions: How would you handle the case if you were a tour leader?

Comments:

(1)_____

(2)_____

(3)_____

 扫一扫，有答案。

 小知识

下榻酒店后领队的工作

1. 与地陪一起向总服务台提供团名、团队名单、团队签证，提出住房要求，协助地陪办理入住登记手续。
2. 分配住房，领队应掌握分房名单，并与地陪相互告知各自的房号和联系电话，以便协调工作。
3. 引领客人和行李进房，巡视客人的住房状态，询问客人是否拿到自己的行李，对房间是否满意。
4. 提醒客人晚上出去的时候一定要结伴而行，带上宾馆的联系方式，告诉游客附近商店的位置。
5. 与前台联系，定好叫早时间，协助客人解决入住后遇到的各种问题。如遇卫生问题、房间内设施问题，及时通知前台；如拿错行李或行李未到，协同地陪一起处理。

Part Two Listening Comprehension
第二部分：听力训练

Words and Expressions

chains	n.	连锁企业	oversea	adj.	外国的；海外的
quality	n.	品质	inadequate	adj.	不充分的
closet	n.	壁橱	stipulate	v.	规定；保证
generally	adv.	一般地	staff	n.	职员
turnaround	n.	转变；转向	single	adj.	单一的
indicate	vt.	表明；指出	formality	n.	正式手续

Service after Check-in 入住酒店后的服务

1. Listen to the passage and fill in the blanks with the missing information you have heard.

 扫一扫，听一听。

A tour leader should offer the following services to the tourists when he takes them to the hotel:

(1) Inform the tourists of the _____ .

(2) _____ and tell tourists how to use them.

(3) If tourists request a change of rooms because of the inadequate facilities, the tour leader should ask the hotel staff to _____ which are stipulated in the contract.

(4) If tourists ask for a suite instead of the single room and _____, the tour leader can help through the formalities.

 扫一扫，有答案。

2. Listen to the passage again, and try to give correspondent English version and put the sentences in the correct order.

_____ 如果客房设施存在缺陷，客人要求调换房间，导游应要求酒店工作人员按合同规定更换客房，满足游客的要求。

_____ 告知海外游客当地时间。

_____ 检查客房设施并告诉游客使用方法。

_____ 如果客人要求入住套房替换原来已订的单人房，并愿意支付房费差价，导游可以协助办理。

扫一扫，有答案。

Part Three Situational Dialogue
第三部分：情景对话

Task 6-1 Check-in 入住酒店

Bell Service 行李交接服务

1. Listen to the dialogue and fill in the blanks with the missing words or phrases you've just heard.

 扫一扫，听一听。

(T=Tour Leader; P=Porter)

P: Good afternoon. Let me take care of your luggage.

T: Thank you! Be careful! Things inside the bag are fragile. (1)_____.

P: No worries! Here we are. May I have your key card?

T: Here you are.

P: Thank you! Would you please (2)_____?

T: Certainly. I'll ask our tour members to keep them in the safe.

P: With pleasure. Feel free to let me know should (3)_____.

T: Thanks a lot!

 扫一扫，有答案。

2. Listen again, and do a situational dialogue with your partner.

Task 6-2 Concierge 礼宾服务

Keeping Valuables 保管贵重物品

1. Listen to the dialogue and answer the following questions.

 扫一扫，听一听。

(1) What valuables are there in his bag?
_____

(2) How long will the bag be kept?
_____

(3) When will the cloakroom close?
_____

 扫一扫，有答案。

2. Role play: One student plays the role of the tour leader while another plays the role of the Bellman of Cloakroom.

Task 6-3 Inquires in the Hotel 店内问询

Inquires about City Tour 询问市内观光旅游

1. Listen to the dialogue and choose the best answer according to the information you've heard.

 扫一扫，听一听。

(1) What is the man doing? ____
    A. He is asking the information about the city tour.
    B. He is visiting the Museum of Modern Art.
    C. He is walking.
    D. He is having dinner.

(2) We can learn from the passage that ____.
    A. There are no free maps of the city.
    B. The clerk is so rude.
    C. It won't take you more than twenty minutes to the Museum of Modern Art on foot.
    D. The tour leader will check out the hotel this evening.

 扫一扫，有答案。

2. Role play: Suppose you are a tour leader and your classmate is the clerk of the information desk. Ask him the information about the city tour.

Task 6-4 Laundry Service 洗衣服务

Inquires about Laundry Service 询问洗衣服务

1. Listen to the dialogue and fill in the blanks with the missing words or phrases you've just heard.

扫一扫，听一听。

(F=Floor Attendant; T=Tour leader)

F: (1) Laundry service, _____?

T: Come in, please.

F: Good morning, sir. (2) _____?

T: No, not now. Thank you.

F: Well, if you have any, Please leave it in the laundry bag (3) _____ . I come to collect it every morning.

T: Thank you. But how long does it usually take (4) _____ if I send it?

F: Well, we offer express service and same-day, it depends on which service (5) _____ .

T: Any difference in price?

F: Yes, sir. We charge 50% more for express, but it only takes 5 hours.

T: What about same-day? Can I get it back in the evening?

F: Certainly, sir. All deliveries will be made (6) _____ .

T: Oh, I see. Thanks a lot.

F: You are welcome.

扫一扫，有答案。

2. Role play: One student plays the role of tour leader while the other plays the role of floor attendant.

Part Four ABC about Destination Countries
第四部分：目的地国家概况

New Zealand 新西兰

  New Zealand is an island nation in the southwestern Pacific Ocean. The capital city is Wellington while its most populous city is Auckland. The country geographically comprises two main land masses—the North Island and the South Island. The country's varied topography and its sharp mountain peaks, such as the Southern Alps, owe much to the tectonic (地壳构造的) uplift of land and volcanic eruptions. The subtropical Northland region stretches upwards from Auckland to the very top of New Zealand. It is known for its diverse natural beauty that includes a mixture of white-sand beaches, forests of giant Kauri (贝壳杉) trees, picturesque islands and huge sand dunes.

  Christianity (基督教) is the predominant religion in New Zealand. In the 2013 census, 55.0% of the population identified with one or more religions, including 49.0% identifying as Christians. Another 41.9% indicated that they had no religion. English is the predominant language, spoken by 96.1% of the population. After the Second World War, Māori (毛利人) were discouraged from speaking their own language in schools and workplaces and it existed as a community language only in a few remote areas.

  You would never think that a country nestled in the corner of the world would be so multi-cultural, but you really don't realize how different it is until you arrive. There are literally people from all over the world that live in New Zealand. Māori were the first to arrive in New Zealand, journeying in canoes (独木舟) from Hawaii (夏威夷) about 1,000 years ago. There are many Asians and Africans who have also immigrated to the country over the years, making it a literal melting pot of cultures.

  So, as you can see, the culture in New Zealand is full of very interesting and unique (独特的) people that you can't find anywhere else in the world. Because of their friendliness, which is so different from what you will see in your own country, you will feel like you've arrived at home, even though you may be thousands of miles away. You should take the time to learn more about them before you go to the country.

Read the passage aloud and choose the best answer to complete each statement.

1. The varied topography of New Zealand and its sharp mountain peaks owe much to _____.
  A. earthquakes   B. tsunamis
  C. sand dunes   D. tectonic uplift of land

2. Most of the New Zealanders are immigrants from European countries who believe in _____.

   A. Catholicism   B. Buddhism

   C. Christianity   D. totems

3. Based on the text, which of the following statements is NOT true correct? _____.

   A. Asians and Africans also immigrated to New Zealand, making it a literal melting pot of cultures.

   B. Most of the New Zealanders are very friendly and polite, but Māori are exceptions.

   C. More than 90% of the New Zealanders speak English, but Māori speak their local dialect.

   D. Māori were the first to arrive in New Zealand, and they came in canoes from Hawaii.

4. _____ is known for its diverse natural beauty that includes a mixture of white-sand beaches, forests of giant Kauri trees, picturesque islands and huge sand dunes.

   A. Auckland   B. Wellington

   C. South Island   D. Northland region

扫一扫，有答案。

Watch the short video twice, and complete the following requirements.

Step 1:   Watch the video and take notes of what you have watched or heard. Compare the notes with your desk mate.

Step 2:   Watch the video again and fill in the blanks in the following sentences with what you have watched or heard.

   Summary:

   1. Nicknamed the city of _____, Auckland has more boats per capita than anywhere else in the world.

   2. As the country's biggest city, Auckland has modern walls, spacious, _____ parks, and plenty of culture.

   3. Unspoiled nature, Auckland's rugged coastline with _____ cliffs, and rolling hills is simply stunning.

   4. Just before _____, hike or drive to the top of Mount Eden, an inner-city volcano to see the sparkling lights reveal some of the city's finest buildings.

   5. The appeal is still there today and the city's unique history, untouched nature, family friendly _____, and easygoing lifestyle make it a desired destination for millions of overseas visitors every year.

 扫一扫，看视频。

Part Five Consolidation
第五部分：巩固练习

Practical Writing 应用文写作

Hotel Registration Card
酒店入住登记卡

Whether a hotel is booked through an online travel provider, a travel agent or directly with hotel staff, understanding the details of hotel registration will help ensure you a pleasant stay. Any incorrect information listed on the hotel registration may affect service quality of the hotel as well as your experience when you stay in the hotel.

Suppose you are the guest, fill out the registration card of Holiday Inn Crown Plaza and deliver it to the Front Desk clerk. Don't hesitate to ask the receptionist if you have any problems when you fill in the registration form.

Outline:

(1) Name of the guest
(2) Gender
(3) Nationality
(4) Passport number
(5) Private address
(6) Others

Chapter 6
下榻酒店
Hotel Check-in

Translation for the Tour Leader 领队翻译

1. Translate the following sentences into English with the words or phrases given.

(1) 对不起，我们已经客满了。但是我可以介绍您去东方(Orient Hotel)饭店，那里有空余(spare room)的房间。
(2) 请告诉我们或在洗衣单上写明您的洗衣服务需求如熨烫(ironed)、水洗(washed)、干洗(dry-cleaned) 或是缝补(mended)，还要写明何时需要取衣服。
(3) 我们有中餐厅(Chinese restaurant)和西餐厅(western-style restaurant)，您愿意去哪个？
(4) 我们有理发室(barber shop)、洗衣房(laundry)、小卖部(store)、邮电服务 (telegram services)、报刊供应柜(newspaper stand)、弹子房(billiard)、乒乓球和电子游戏。
(5) 酒店规定(stipulates)在房间内不能使用客人自带的电器(electric appliances)，我们在您住店期间可以为您保存。

扫一扫，做翻译。

2. Translate the following sentences into Chinese with the words or phrases given.

(1) For local telephone (本地电话) calls, please press 9 first and then dial the number.
(2) I'm sorry, we don't have any single rooms left, would you like a double room (双人间)?
(3) Four nights at 90 US dollars each, and here are the meals (膳食) that you had at the hotel. That makes a total of 665 US dollars.
(4) I'd like to book a single room with bath (浴室) from the after-noon of October 4 to the morning of October 10.
(5) At what time would you like us to call (叫醒) you tomorrow morning?

扫一扫，做翻译。

本章参考文献

[1]曹银玲. 出境领队实务[M]. 北京：旅游教育出版社，2012.
[2]王远梅. 空乘英语[M]. 北京：国防工业出版社，2010.
[3]王健民. 出境旅游领队实务[M]. 5版. 北京：旅游教育出版社，2016.

[4]黄恢月，仇向明. 出境旅游领队工作案例解析[M]. 北京：旅游教育出版社，2008.
[5]袁智敏，仇向明. 领队英语[M]. 2版. 北京：旅游教育出版社，2008.
[6] http://v.youku.com/v_show/id_XMjY2NzI4Njk3Ng==.html

Chapter 7

观光娱乐
Sightseeing and Recreation

Learning Focus 学习要点

- **Case Study**
  Getting Lost
- **Listening Comprehension**
  Concert Tickets
- **Situational Dialogue**
  Task 7-1 Sightseeing
  　　　　—Bus Tour
  　　　　—Introduction to Tourist Attraction by a Local Guide
  Task 7-2 Recreational Activities
  　　　　—Bowling
  　　　　—Nightclub
  Task 7-3 Other Entertainments
  　　　　—Museums
  　　　　—Theme Parks
- **ABC about Destination Countries**
  ABC about France
- **Consolidation**
  Practical Writing: Advertisement
  Translation for Tour Leader

- **案例分析**
  迷路了
- **听力训练**
  音乐会门票
- **情景对话**
  ①观光旅游
  　　——巴士旅游
  　　——地陪景点讲解
  ②娱乐活动
  　　——保龄球
  　　——夜总会
  ③其他娱乐活动
  　　——博物馆
  　　——主题公园
- **目的地国家概况**
  法国概况
- **巩固练习**
  应用文写作：广告
  领队翻译

Part One Case Study
第一部分：案例分析

Getting Lost 迷路了

It was Mr. Ren's tenth wedding anniversary. The couple decided to travel in Vancouver, Canada for a celebration. Having compared several travel agencies, they decided to join a Seven-day Romantic Tour of Sleepless Vancouver launched by a well-known domestic travel agency. The tour members are all couples or lovers, having a dream to enjoy their sweet time in Canada.

One day, after they visited the attractions specified in the travel schedule, the tour leader suggested they go back to the hotel. All tour members agreed. Having arrived at the hotel, they felt tired. Some of them splashed water in the swimming pool for relaxation while others went back to their rooms for a rest. Mr. Ren, however, intended to buy a gift for his wife to commemorate their wedding anniversary. He came up to the tour leader and said: "We'd like go out shopping, Mr. Zhang." The tour leader replied: "OK, but please come back before dinner time." They gave a nod as a signal of consent, and then went out together.

The couple arrived at a large shopping mall near the hotel by taxi, shopping from one store to another. After hours, they came to know that they had got lost. They tried hard to find the familiar buildings that could direct them back to the hotel, but in vain. Then, they tried to take a taxi, but the taxi driver could not help because they forgot taking the hotel card with them. They tried to recall the hotel's name, but neither of them could remember it. What could they do?

When they were in trouble, it happened that somebody hailed them. It was Ricky, an overseas Chinese businessman who lived in the same hotel. Luckily enough, he could speak Chinese. Knowing what had happened to the couple, he said: "I am going back to the hotel. Come on with me." When they got to the hotel, Mr. Ren expressed his thanks to Ricky again and again. Ricky told him, "When you go out next time, please take the hotel card with you. The taxi driver will take you to your hotel if you get lost."

 扫一扫，看译文。

Chapter 7

观光娱乐
Sightseeing and Recreation

1. Study the case carefully. Decide whether the following statements are true or false and write T for true and F for false.

(1) _____ The tour leader should not arrange any free activities after they finish visiting the sites according to the travel schedule.

(2) _____ The tour leader should stay with all tour members when they have free activities.

(3) _____ The tour leader made a mistake because he allowed the couple to go shopping alone.

(4) _____ The tour leader is to blame although he has reminded the couple of coming back before dinner time.

(5) _____ The tour leader should pay Ricky because he sent the couple back to the hotel.

 扫一扫，有答案。

2. Divide the class into several groups for a brief discussion. One student makes a presentation of the main points discussed and the others give comments on the presentation.

Discussions: What can a tour leader do to prevent tourists from getting lost?
Comments:
(1)_____
(2)_____
(3)_____
(4)_____
(5)_____

 扫一扫，有答案。

 小知识

游览中领队的工作

1. 在前往景点的途中，导游向游客介绍当地的风土人情、自然景观，回答游客提出的问题；抵达景点后，向游客详细讲解该景点，尤其是景点的历史价值和特色。领队应监督当地导游完成这项工作。

2. 游览过程中，领队应随时清点人数，以防游客走失。领队的站位，应该始终是在团队的最后，与导游形成首尾呼应。

3. 因交通、天气的原因调整旅游行程，领队在与导游进行磋商后，应将调整后的日程及时通知到每一位旅游者，并征得其同意。

Part Two Listening Comprehension
第二部分：听力训练

Words and Expressions

architectural	adj.	建筑上的	landmark	n.	地标
glance	n.	一瞥	depict	v.	描述
acoustics	n.	音响效果	unparalleled	adj.	无与伦比的
ticket broker		票务代理	cancel	v.	取消
refund	n.	退款	counterfeit	adj.	假冒的

Concert Tickets 音乐会门票

1. Listen to the dialogue and fill in the blanks with the missing information you've heard.

 扫一扫，听一听。

Walt Disney Concert Hall is one of the best (1)_____ in the world, and its building is regarded as an internationally architectural (2) _____. When coming to have a glance at it, you may depict it with two words: unique and (3) _____. The construction cost is also the highest. The acoustics is very magnificent, and the musical experience in it is (4) _____. If you have a chance to enjoy a live concert there, it must be an (5) _____ experience. But it is hard to get tickets there. To get the tickets, you may surf its website to see what programs are on, book tickets (6) _____ or over the phone. If all tickets have been sold out, you can check newspaper classified ads or other online user-to-user sales areas, or even contact a ticket (7) _____for sold out tickets. If the concert is canceled, you cannot get the (8) _____. And you should also be careful because some people may sell (9)_____ tickets.

 扫一扫，有答案。

2. Fill in the blanks with the words and expressions given below and change their forms when necessary.

88

Chapter 7

观光娱乐
Sightseeing and Recreation

| attractive | over | sell out | magnificence | expensive |
| counterfeiting | landmark | height | classify | living |

(1) The building they've just passed by differs from others and_____ people' attentions.

(2) It is one of the world-best concert halls and is regard as an international _____.

(3) The expense of the building is_____ than other similar buildings.

(4) You can enjoy the unparalleled musical experience because of its_____ acoustics.

(5) To enjoy a_____ concert will be an unforgettable experience.

(6) People could search its website to see what programs are on and book tickets online or_____ the phone.

(7) What measures we should take if all tickets already have been_____.

(8) Checking newspaper _____ads is a good way to look for some sold out tickets.

(9) Those tickets bought from such ways are less_____ than their face value.

(10) Please be careful because _____ tickets will get you into trouble.

扫一扫，有答案。

Part Three Situational Dialogue
第三部分：情景对话

Words and Expressions

transit	n.	中转	transfer	v.	转乘
escort	v.	护送	stamp	n.	印章
icon	n.	符号	posture	n.	姿势
foul line		边线	cradle	v.	怀抱
retract	v.	缩回	bartender	n.	酒吧侍者
jukebox	n.	自动唱机	speakeasy	n.	非法经营的酒吧

Task 7-1 Sightseeing 观光旅游

Bus Tour 巴士旅游

1. Listen to the dialogue and write numbers in the blanks to show the correct order of the conversation.

扫一扫，听一听。

(D=Driver;   L=Tour Leader)

____(1) **D:** Hello, will you get on?

____(2) **D:** Yes, get on please.

____(3) **T:** Thank you so much!

____(4) **D:** Transfer to bus No. 2 when we get to Downtown Transit Center. Here are maps. Feel free to take one with you.

____(5) **T:** Excuse me, sir. I want to go to the Gallery. How could I get there?

____(6) **D:** One dollar. Put it into the slot. Since you have to transfer, I will give you a Q Card. So you can transfer any bus number without paying extra fare within two hours.

____(7) **D:** Please push the stop button when it reaches your stop.

____(8) **T:** Hello, is the bus to Downtown Transit Center?

____(9) **T:** Thanks. It's very kind of you.

____(10) **T:** Thank you. And how much is the fare?

____(11) **T:** I'm escorting a tour group. Would you please remind me when we reach Downtown Transit Center?

____(12) **D:** No problem. You can take a look at the schedule on your map.

扫一扫，有答案。

2. Listen to the dialogue again, and act it out with your deskmate. Pay attention to your body language.

Introduction to Tourist Attraction by a Local Guide 地陪景点讲解

1. Listen to the dialogue and complete the following sentences in your own words.

 扫一扫，听一听。

(1) The local guide will escort tourists to discover _____.

(2) The postcard will have a special stamp on it, _____.

(3) The Eiffel Tower is the landmark of Paris, and also _____.

Chapter 7
观光娱乐
Sightseeing and Recreation

(4) It was erected in 1889. Since then, it has become _____.

(5) The height of the Eiffel Tower is _____, the same height as an _____ _____.

 扫一扫，有答案。

2. Role play: Listen to the dialogue again and act it out with your partner using information you've heard.

Task 7-2 Recreational Activities 娱乐活动

Bowling 保龄球

1. Listen to the dialogue and answer the following questions.

 扫一扫，听一听。

(1) What is the most important aspect a player should follow?
_____

(2) Is the right posture very important for a player? How can he keep the right posture?
_____

(3) Why should the player look at the pins when delivering the ball?
_____

(4) Where should the player stand on the approach?
_____

(5) What is the proper way for a player to release the ball?
_____

 扫一扫，有答案。

2. Role play: One student plays the role of the coach while another plays the role of the tour leader. Show how to play bowling to the tour members.

Nightclub 夜总会

1. Listen to the dialogue and put the following responses in the correct order.

91

扫一扫，听一听。

Bartender	Tour Leader
(1) Welcome to Pure Nightclub Las-Vegas. What can I do for you?	A. Yes. It's amazing. We like the electronic dance music, disco, house and hip hop and so on. And the lively atmosphere makes us so relaxed.
(2) Ok, here you are. Is this your first time to come here? What about it?	B. Of course. I'm very glad to talk with you. See you.
(3) Wow, you know the club well. Eh, from about 1900 to 1920, Americans would gather at honky tonks or juke joints to dance to music played on a piano or a jukebox. It is the original form of the nightclub.	C. I am not clear about it, either. I think at that time, people couldn't embrace the edgy entertainment.
(4) Yes, but I still don't know the reasons for prohibition. Do you know?	D. Thanks. Give us the most popular wine in your club.
(5) I agree with you. Please enjoy yourself.	E. Great. But once upon a time, it was forbidden and went underground as illegal speakeasy bars.

扫一扫，有答案。

2. Divide the class into groups of two or three students, and make the dialogue again.

Task 7-3 Other Entertainments 其他娱乐活动

Museums 博物馆

1. Listen to the dialogue and pick up the right picture based on the information you have heard.

Chapter 7
观光娱乐
Sightseeing and Recreation

 扫一扫，听一听。

A B C

 扫一扫，有答案。

2. Listen to the dialogue again and do a situational dialogue with your partner.

Theme Parks 主题公园

1. Listen to the dialogue and fill in the blanks with correct information.

 扫一扫，听一听。

(1) Name of the pirate ship: _____

(2) The entertainment item: _____

(3) The reason for the fear of the ride: _____

(4) The reason for taking the ride: _____

 扫一扫，有答案。

2. Role play with your partner. One student plays the role of the tour leader while another plays the role of a tour member. Role-play the dialogue again.

93

Part Four ABC about Destination Countries
第四部分：目的地国家概况

France 法国

France lies in the heart of Europe with a total area of 551,000 square kilometers and a population of 57,500,000. French borders on Italy, Switzerland and Monaco (摩纳哥) in the east and Germany, Belgium (比利时) and Luxembourg (卢森堡公国) in the northeast and Spain, Andorra (安道尔共和国) in the southwest and England to the northwest. French is symmetrical hexagon (六边形). Basically French is a plain country. 80% of its territory is plain and hill. Plain land at an elevation(海拔) of below 250 meters is about 60% of its total areas. Hills between 200 to 250 are about 20% while more than 500 is about 20%. The terrain (地形) is low in northwest and high in southeast.

Paris is the capital and most populous city of France. The centre of Paris contains the most visited monuments in the city, including Notre Dame de Paris (巴黎圣母院) and the Louvre Museum (卢浮宫) as well as Church Sainte-Chapelle (圣礼拜堂), The National Residence of the Invalides (巴黎荣军院), where the tomb of Napoleon (拿破仑墓) is located. The Eiffel Tower (埃菲尔铁塔) is located on the Left Bank south-west of the centre, and other landmarks are laid out east to west along the historical axis of Paris. For centuries, Paris has attracted artists from around the world, who arrive in the city to educate themselves and to seek inspiration from its vast pool of artistic resources and galleries. As a result, Paris has acquired a reputation as the "City of Art".

When talking about France, we can't ignore the culture of French food and drink. The food and drink in France enjoys a long lasting fame for its long history, various and dainty (精致的) kinds, and unique character. Its cooking skills are the second to none among the western style food, of which the French feel proud. In terms of drink, what the French like most is grape wine. When they have a meal, the French will pay much attention to the match of dainty cakes and wine, such as meat with red grape wine, fish with white grape wine and so on. Besides, Frenchmen are fond of cheeses with different tastes. Its consumption quantity ranks first in the world, therefore France was given the name of "Kingdom of Cheese".

France is the first tourism country in the world. It has 37 sites inscribed in UNESCO's World Heritage List and features cities of high cultural interest, beaches and seaside resorts, ski resorts (滑雪胜地), and rural regions that many enjoy for their beauty and tranquility (green tourism). Small and picturesque French villages are promoted through the association Les Plus Beaux Villages de France ("The Most Beautiful Villages of France"). The "Remarkable Gardens" label is a list of the over 200 gardens classified by the French Ministry of Culture. This label is intended to protect and promote remarkable gardens and parks. In this romantic country, you can enjoy famous snacks and grape wine, at the same time you can also enjoy beautiful rural scenery (田园风光) or significant Medieval castle (中世纪城堡) or the joy of skiing in snowcapped Alps or you may swim in the attractive blue sea and feel the glamour (魅力) of this romantic capital which is filled with cultural and modern taste.

Read the passage aloud and choose the best answer to complete each statement.

1. France lies in the heart of Europe and borders on_____.

A. Italy, Switzerland and Monaco in the southeast

B. Germany, Belgium and Luxembourg in the northeast

C. Spain, Monaco and Luxembourg in the southwest

D. England, Andorra and Switzerland to the northwest

2. The centre of Paris contains the most visited monuments in the city, including _____.

A. the Eiffel Tower

B. Musée du Louvre

C. Notre Dame Cathedral

D. Les Plus Beaux Villages de France

3. Based on the text, which of the following statements is NOT true?

A. The tourists enjoy the rural regions of France for their beauty and tranquility.

B. French terrain is low in northwest and high in southeast with a long coastline in the east.

C. There are a lot of cultural heritage sites and many tourist activities in France.

D. For its long history, the food and drink in France enjoys a long lasting fame.

4. We can infer from the passage that _____

A. France is a tourism country which attracts a great number of tourists from around the world.

B. The French are pound of their cooking skills which are the best among the western style food.

C. France is reputed as the "Kingdom of Cheese", and love cheese with different tastes.

D. Paris has acquired a reputation as the "City of Remarkable Gardens" for its numerous gardens.

 扫一扫，有答案。

Watch the short video twice, and complete the following requirements.

Step 1:   Watch the video and take notes of what you have watched or heard. Compare the notes with your desk mate.

Step 2: Watch the video again and fill in the blanks in the following sentences with what you have watched or heard.

Summary:

1. Tourists are particularly attracted to the Verdon Gorge because it's so close to the French Riviera, and because of the _____ activities available there like hiking, kayaking, and rock climbing.

2. The Palace of Versailles is most famous for being the site of the palace of Versailles, a _____ chateau with strong roots in French history.

3. One of the most famous and most distinctive _____ in the city, Arc de Triomphe has got roots from both the French Revolution and the Napoleonic wars.

4. Not only is the exterior of Notre-Dame de Paris breathtaking, the interior boasts all the makings of a _____ Gothic church, even the basement has a fascinating history.

5. Eiffel Tower is not only the world's most visited monument, but also an _____ of the country which stands over 1000 feet tall.

 扫一扫，看视频。

Part Five Consolidation
第五部分：巩固练习

Practical Writing 应用文写作

Advertisement 广告

No matter how great your hotel or nightclub is, no one will ever know unless you advertise it. Write concisely, yet truthfully. Make sure to use selling adjectives such as "best", "great", "excellent" and "effective". Think about the possibility of offering a first time incentive. A free sample, trial or even a money-back guarantee will draw customers to your product. You may invite guests to taste some new tea, or you may allow them to enjoy the new liquor with 50% discount. In order to spark the interest of your regular guests, you may also offer them a few free bottles of wines.

Suppose you're the manager of the nightclub in the hotel, write an advertisement to promote the beverage in your restaurant.

Outline:

(1) Names of the discounted wine or liquor 打折酒品名

(2) The features of each wine or liquor 酒的特征

(3) Location of the nightclub 夜店位置

(4) Service hours 营业时间

(5) How to make reservations (Tel. No.) 如何预订(电话：××××)

Translation for the Tour Leader 领队翻译

1. Translate the following sentences into English with the words or phrases given.

(1) 黄石国家公园是美国最大、最负盛名(foremost)的国家公园。它最吸引人的地方之一在于它的喷泉。

(2) 请记住，在这儿过马路要先看右边(look to the right)，而不是像你们国家往左看，所以一定要注意。

(3) 在少数民族(ethnic minorities)地区旅游，你不但能观赏到美丽的风景，还能领略到当地的民俗和传统文化。

(4) 卢浮宫(Louvre)每个月第一个星期日免费开放。

(5) 每个项目都有一个售票亭(a ticket booth)。您可以在那里买票。

扫一扫，做翻译。

2. Translate the following sentences into Chinese with the words or phrases given.

(1) To pick up a map as soon as you enter the museum and take a few moments to acquaint yourself with(熟悉) the exhibits and layout.

(2) Westminster Abbey is not only a church and the place where monarchs (君主) are crowned but also the rest place of famous statesmen, scientists, poets and musicians.

(3) You can check newspaper classified ads (分类广告)or other online user-to-user sales areas, even contact a ticket broker.

(4) By the way, can I take the tram (电车) free by the admission ticket? I forgot taking pocket money with me.

(5) The concert hall is in Tivoli. We can spend the day playing in the park and then catch a concert there at night.

扫一扫，做翻译。

本章参考文献

[1] 曹景洲. 海外旅游领队业务[M]. 北京：中国旅游出版社，2011.
[2] 王健民. 出境旅游领队实务[M]. 5版. 北京：旅游教育出版社，2016.
[3] 李娌, 王哲. 导游服务案例精选解析[M]. 北京：旅游教育出版社，2007.
[4] http://wenku.baidu.com/view/13737003de80d4d8d15a4f20.html
[5] http://www.en8848.com.cn/kouyu/live/shdh/181346.html
[6] http://www.kekenet.com/kouyu/201311/264772.shtml
[7] https://zhidao.baidu.com/question/67936319.html
[8] http://www.watchmojo.com/index_template.php?template=template_archive_2011&type=id&content=12607&rule=2

Chapter 8

购物与自由活动
Shopping and Free Activities

Learning Focus 学习要点

- ◆ **Case Study**
  An Unpleasant Shopping
- ◆ **Listening Comprehension**
  Shopping Tips
- ◆ **Situational Dialogue**
  Task 8-1 Shopping Abroad
  　　　　　—At the Duty-free Shop
  Task 8-2 Public Transportation
  　　　　　—Taking Subways
  　　　　　—Taking Taxis
  Task 8-3 Bars and Restaurants
  　　　　　—At the Restaurant
  　　　　　—Footing the Bill
  Task 8-4 Others
  　　　　　—At the Post Office
  　　　　　—Currency Exchange
- ◆ **ABC about Destination Countries**
  ABC about Italy
- ◆ **Consolidation**
  Practical Writing: Exchange Form
  Translation for Tour Leader

- ◆ 案例分析
  不愉快的购物
- ◆ 听力训练
  购物小窍门
- ◆ 情景对话
  ①境外购物
  　——在免税店
  ②公共交通
  　——乘坐地铁
  　——乘坐计程车
  ③酒吧和餐馆
  　——在餐馆
  　——付账
  ④其他事项
  　——在邮局
  　——货币兑换
- ◆ 目的地国家概况
  意大利概况
- ◆ 巩固练习
  应用文写作：兑换单
  领队翻译

Part One Case Study
第一部分：案例分析

An Unpleasant Shopping
不愉快的购物

Ms. Yang joined a seven-day tour to Thailand. The tour leader claimed that he would provide tourists with good service and protect their interests. If they had any request, he would do his best to help. The tour leader went well with the tourists during the trip.

One day, while shopping in a shopping mall, the tour leader tried to recommend jewelry to the tour members and helped them to select the products. He vigorously promoted the jewelry, saying how cheap and beautiful they were. At his advice, the tourists bought a lot of jewelry.

Back in China, Ms. Yang was worried about the jewelry's quality. He entrusted a jewelry test center to appraise the jewels she bought, and some of them turned out to be defective products. Ms. Yang requested the travel service for a compensation, but it did not work. Then, she reported the matter to the relevant administration. After investigation, the administration ordered the travel service to do an apology and compensate for Ms. Yang. In addition, the administration conducted administrative penalty on the travel service.

 扫一扫，看译文。

1. Study the case carefully. Decide whether the following statements are true or false and write T for true and F for false.

(1) _____ The tour leader would be kind to the tourists all the way and claimed that he would protect the interests of tourists.

(2) _____ The tour leader said that he would try his best to meet the demands the tourists proposed.

(3) _____ During the shopping time, the tour leader recommended perfect-quality merchandise to tourists.

(4) _____ The jewels recommended by the tour leader were accordance with their real value as the tour leader said.

(5) _____ Ms. Yang asked a jewelry appraisal testing center to identify the jewels, however, there were flaws.

Chapter 8

购物与自由活动
Shopping and Free Activities

 扫一扫，有答案。

2. Divide the class into several groups for a brief discussion. One student makes a presentation of the main points discussed and the others give comments on the presentation.

Discussions: What could the tour leader do when tourists make some shopping?
Comments:
(1) _____
(2) _____
(3) _____

 扫一扫，有答案。

 小知识

购物时领队的工作

1. 领队应监督导游安排购物次数。如导游拟增加购物次数，事先须与领队商量，并且必须征得游客的同意。
2. 领队应向游客介绍本地商品的特色、讲清购物停留时间、介绍购物的有关注意事项。
3. 领队应随时向游客提供在购物过程中所需要的服务，如语言翻译、介绍托运手续等。
4. 领队应了解欧洲国家的退税规定，提前向游客介绍。在游客到商店购物时，提醒游客别忘记要发票。
5. 商店不按质论价、抛售伪劣商品、不提供标准服务时，领队应出面与商店交涉，以维护游客的利益不受侵害。

Part Two Listening Comprehension
第二部分：听力训练

Words and Expressions

bargain	n.	减价货	blowout	n.	盛大聚会
promotional	adj.	促销的	off-price	adj.	廉价的
couture	n.	时装	mark down		降价

Shopping Tips 购物小窍门

1. Listen to the passage and fill in the blanks with the missing information you have heard.

 扫一扫，听一听。

Who doesn't love a great bargain? From an in-store sale to an end of year blowout, department stores frequently provide discount and (1) _____ to encourage shoppers to spend. With the right information, you don't need to shop less, just (2) _____. With the right tips to help you bargain shop, you can still look good and feel good without breaking the bank.

For label lovers, off-price stores offer heavily discounted designer and brand-name items direct from (3) _____. Here you can find couture brands from Fendi all the way to Calvin Klein and Juicy Couture at heavily (4) _____. For those who are not particularly concerned with brand names, head to your local (5) _____ such as Target, Kmart or Walmart. These days, chain stores are stocking excellent basics such as denim, shirts, underwear and simple business attire.

As with anything in life, timing is everything. You can catch (6) _____ during holidays. If you go shopping during these days, you will likely notice they sometimes hold "25% off," "take an extra 10% off" or "buy one, get one half off" sales to make room for new stock. If you shop during a sale, you can find items up to 70 percent off of (7) _____. This will allow you to still get the products you love but for a much cheaper price.

 扫一扫，有答案。

Chapter 8
购物与自由活动
Shopping and Free Activities

2. Fill in the blanks with the words and expressions given below and change their forms when necessary.

| discount | tip | promotion | sell |
| stock | frequent | chain | |

(1) Tourists will find that department stores _____ provide discount to encourage them to spend.

(2) With the right shopping _____, tourists can still look good and feel good when they are shopping.

(3) For label lovers, off-price stores offer heavily _____ brand-name items direct from department stores.

(4) _____ stores are stocking excellent basics such as shirts, underwear and simple business.

(5) As with anything in life, timing is everything for the tourists. They can get cheaper products during the _____ events.

(6) Sometimes department stores hold "25% off," "take an extra 10% off" or "buy one, get one half off" sales to make room for new _____.

(7) Tourists can get the products they love but for a much cheaper price during a _____.

 扫一扫，有答案。

Part Three Situational Dialogue
第三部分：情景对话

Words and Expressions

cosmetic	n.	化妆品	perfume	n.	香水
Burberry	n.	巴宝莉	Lancôme	n.	兰蔻
fragrance	n.	芳香剂	intercontinental	n.	摩天楼
Embraer	n.	巴西航空工业公司	authentic	adj.	真正的
vermouth	n.	苦艾酒	equivalent	adj.	相等的

Task 8-1 Shopping Abroad 境外购物

At the Duty-free Shop 在免税店

1. Listen to the dialogue and write numbers in the blanks to show the correct order of the conversation.

 扫一扫，听一听。

(T= Tour Leader; S=Shop Assistant)

_____(1) **S:** My pleasure.

_____(2) **T:** Please pack it for her. Thank you.

_____(3) **S:** Good morning, sir.

_____(4) **T:** Yes, how much is this?

_____(5) **S:** There are toys, story books and Barbie. Which one does she want?

_____(6) **T:** Good morning, miss. What do you have for us?

_____(7) **S:** 35 dollars.

_____(8) **T:** Do you have anything for children? This lady wants to buy a gift for her daughter.

_____(9) **S:** OK, do you like this one? This style is popular among the people. Many tourists would like to take it as their souvenirs.

_____(10) **T:** She said she'd like to have the Barbie.

_____(11) **S:** We have a broad selection of affordable high quality products. Our catalogue includes cosmetics and fragrances for men and women, gift items for adults and children, confectionery, and jewelry.

 扫一扫，有答案。

2. Listen to the dialogue again, and act it out with your deskmate. Pay attention to your body language.

Task 8-2 Public Transportation 公共交通

Taking Subways 乘坐地铁

1. Listen to the dialogue carefully and fill in the blanks with information you hear.

 扫一扫，听一听。

Chapter 8
购物与自由活动
Shopping and Free Activities

(T= Tour Leader; C=Clerk)

T: Excuse me.

C: What can I do for you?

T: (1)_____?

C: The pavilion over there.

T: Thank you. I'd like to visit the Statue of Liberty. (2)_____. It seems I can't find the stop in the Metro Instruction Map.

C: (3)_____. And get off at the South Ferry.

T: I see. Thank you very much.

扫一扫，有答案。

2. Pair Work: Make a situational dialogue with your partner.

Taking Taxis 乘坐计程车

1. Listen to the dialogue and put the following responses in the correct order.

扫一扫，听一听。

Tour Leader	Driver
(1) Hey, taxi! Thanks for pulling over	A. You're welcome.
(2) We are going to Broadway.	B. Well. It is quite easy to tell.
(3) Yeah. How did you know?	C. Where to?
(4) Is it that obvious?	D. Is this your first time to the city?

105

(5) Oh, before I forget, can you recommend any good restaurants downtown that offer meals at a reasonable? price?

E. Well, the Mexican restaurant, Peter's, is fantastic. It's not as expensive as other places I know.

(6) Sounds great! Thank you.

F. Well, I can tell tourists from the local people because they walk down the street looking straight up at the skyscrapers.

 扫一扫，有答案。

2. Divide the class into groups of two or three students, and do the dialogue again.

Task 8-3 Bars and Restaurants 酒吧和餐馆

At the Restaurant 在餐馆

1. Listen to the situational dialogue carefully and match the information in column A with that in column B.

 扫一扫，听一听。

Column A	Column B
(1) main course (2) salad (3) drink (4) dessert after meal (5) extra service	A. sparkling mineral water B. a bowl of clam chowder, a wild salmon C. a chocolate cake D. a mixed fruit salad E. a bucket of ice

 扫一扫，有答案。

Chapter 8 购物与自由活动 Shopping and Free Activities

2. Listen to the dialogue again and fill in the blanks with information you hear.

(T=Tour leader; W=Waiter)

W: Good evening, sir. Here is our menu. Would you like (1) _____?
T: Yes, sparkling mineral water, please.
W: No problem. Are you ready to order now, or (2) _____?
T: I'm ready to order now.
W: (3) _____?
T: I'd like to have a bowl of clam chowder, a wild salmon.
W: OK! (4) _____?
T: And a mixed fruit salad please.
W: (5) _____?
T: A chocolate cake, please.
W: (6) _____.
T: Yes. Thank you.
W: Let me repeat your order: a bowl of clam chowder, a wild salmon, a mixed salad and a chocolate cake. (7) _____?
T: Yes. By the way, could you bring me a bucket of ice please?
W: Sure, sir. I'll be right back to you (8)_____.

 扫一扫，有答案。

Footing the Bill 付账

1. Listen to the dialogue and complete the following statements according to the information you have heard.

 扫一扫，听一听。

(1) The tourists had their dinner_____.
(2) The tour leader showed the waiter_____.
(3) The waiter would put the charge_____.
(4) The tourists would check out by_____.

扫一扫，有答案。

107

2. Listen to the dialogue again and choose the right picture which stands for the method of payment.

    A   B   C

 扫一扫，有答案。

Task 8-4 Others 其他事项

At the Post Office 在邮局

1. Listen to the dialogue and fill in blanks with what you've just heard.

 扫一扫，听一听。

    (T=Tour Leader;   S=Staff at the Post Office)

S: Next please! Hello, may I help you, sir?

T: Yes, I want to send (1)_____.

S: OK, it comes to $5.

T: Here is 10 dollars.

S: Here is your change. (2)_____.

T: Here is your receipt. Anything else?

S: (3)_____. This is the notice.

T: Let me see...Hmm…Just a minute.

S: Here it is. (4)_____.

T: Thank you.

 扫一扫，有答案。

2. Role play: One student plays the role of the staff at the post office while

Chapter 8
购物与自由活动
Shopping and Free Activities

another plays the role of the tour leader.

Currency Exchange 货币兑换

1. Listen to the dialogue and mark the following sentences with T (true) and F (false).

 扫一扫，听一听。

(1) _____ The tour leader wanted to cash his personal checks and change some Euros in the hotel.

(2) _____ The tour leader must write his name and passport number on the slip when he wiped his credit card.

(3) _____ The tour leader must present his identity card when he exchanges foreign currencies.

(4) _____ The tour leader was requested to fill in one memo before exchanging US dollars.

(5) _____ The tour leader needed one-dollar notes because he wanted to go shopping in the duty-free shops.

 扫一扫，有答案。

2. Listen to the dialogue again and answer the following questions.

(1) What was the exchange rate on that day?
_____

(2) What should the tour leader write on the memo for exchanging dollars?
_____

(3) What did the cashier remind the tour leader to do after exchange of the money?
_____

(4) What could the tour leader do with the dollars left with him?
_____

 扫一扫，有答案。

Part Four ABC about Destination Countries
第四部分：目的地国家概况

Italy 意大利

Italy is a beautiful country but is one of those countries which you probably have some questions and preconceptions, before your coming to this special country. A place of olive oil (橄榄油), pasta, wine, mafia and sunshine, Roman ruins and renaissance (文艺复兴) palaces, Italy has a lot to give its tourists. Although some of these conceptions are amazing and interesting, it would be a shame if that was the only thing you come away with. Italy is certainly much more complex and stimulating than these concepts.

Italy is a country full of interesting things for the casual tourist and the educated tourist; it has deep Roman Catholic (罗马天主教) roots. The tourists can stay weeks in important tourist centers without reason to feel bored, but it is equally simple to get off the beaten track. In the north, next to the Alps (阿尔卑斯山) and the landscapes of the Po River (波河), many cultural gems (宝石) and highly developed industrial cities fascinate the people all over the world.

Italians are very proud of their cuisine (菜肴) and rightly so, for their food is renowned throughout the world. Italians trace their gastronomic (美食的) heritage to Romans, Greeks, Etruscans (伊特鲁里亚) and other Mediterranean (地中海) peoples who elaborated the methods of raising, refining and preserving foods. Italian cooking is still very regional with the different towns and regions having their own traditions and specialities (特产). Many mouth watering dishes await the intrepid traveller, hundreds of gastronomy specialities, a lot of truly tasty typical products, and all kept very much alive by a modern agricultural system that is careful about preserving the traditional flavours and nutritional values. You will discover a much wider variety of food compared to the dishes often offered in Italian restaurants abroad.

Italy is a land of beauty and glory. The Italians celebrate Christmas and New Year with great pomp (盛况) and show. There are hundreds of festivals held every year in nearly every town in Italy. Celebrations, festivals and street parties are a big part of life in Italy. The bright and colorful festivals in Italy all year round, attract a considerable amount of tourists. Even they too get involved deeply in the multiple hues (色调) of the festive ambience (气氛). Many Italian weekends are spent celebrating food, art, and culture of Italy. Festivals are a way to get in tune with Italian culture. The Italians are more or less always in a festive mood. Every now and then a festive spirit is in the air. The various carnivals, food and wine tasting, Jazz, football, all are parts of the festivities. Italy even hosts a number of international events like, Film Festivals, Dance Festivals and Art Festivals.

Chapter 8

购物与自由活动
Shopping and Free Activities

Read the passage aloud and choose the best answer to complete each statement.

1. Tourists love Italy because it is famous except for _____.
   A. Roman ruins   B. olive oils
   C. mosques   D. renaissance palaces

2. Most of Italians believe in _____ , and you will see some famous religious buildings in Rome.
   A. Christianity   B. Buddhism
   C. Islam   D. Catholicism

3. Which mountain lies in the north of Italy?
   A. the Alps   B. Mont Blanc
   C. the Pyrenees   D. Mount Everest

4. Which of the following statement is Not true?
   A. Italy is complex and stimulating.
   B. Italians are very proud of their agriculture.
   C. Italian food is very ample.
   D. Italy holds hundreds of festivals every year in nearly every town.

扫一扫，有答案。

Watch the short video twice, and complete the following requirements.

Step 1: Watch the video and take notes of what you have watched or heard. Compare the notes with your desk mate.

Step 2: Watch the video again and fill in the blanks in the following sentences with what you have watched or heard.

Summary:

1. In the 17th century _____ European travelers came to Rome searching for the roots of Western civilization.

2. The Colosseum is the most _____ symbol of ancient Rome. Across for four centuries, tens of thousand gladiators, slaves and Christians died in a blaze of glory.

3. The Pantheon was a place to worship all the gods, from Juno, the god of _____, to Mars, the god of war.

4. Once a stadium, today, Piazza Navona is one of Europe's great squares. The thundering crowds and chariots have long faded, _____ by a trio of fountains,

Baroque architectures, artists and the aroma of Rome's best coffee.

5. To really taste all of Rome's treasures can take a _____, but be warmed, it only takes a moment for Rome to forever conquer your heart.

 扫一扫，看视频。

Part Five Consolidation
第五部分：巩固练习

Practical Writing 应用文写作

Exchange Form
兑换单

Depending on where you travel, currency exchange rates can either help you get great bargains or make your trip surprisingly expensive. No matter how strong your home currency is relative to the local currency, however, you want to make sure you're getting the best exchange rate possible whenever you need to get cash or make a purchase. Avoid the exchange companies and Cambio booths that you will see in most train stations and airports. They are convenient, and sometimes (especially in an emergency after banking hours) indispensable, but they frequently charge very high prices in return for the convenience. If you need to get cash, and you can't find an ATM, your best bet is to go to a large bank, post office.

Suppose you are a tourist and fill out the exchange form. Don't hesitate to ask the tour leader if you have any problems when you fill out the form.

Outline:

1. Traveler's Full Name 全名
2. Nationality 国籍
3. Passport No. 护照编号
4. ID. No. 身份证号
5. Full Address in ××× 详细地址
6. Currency 币种
7. Cash Notes 金额
8. Travelers' Checks 旅行支票
9. Bank Checks 银行支票
10. Other 备注
11. For Official Use Only 仅限官方使用
12. Signature of Traveler 游客签字

Chapter 8
购物与自由活动
Shopping and Free Activities

13. Official Seal and Signature 公章及签字
14. Date 日期
15. Date of Conversion 兑换日期
16. Type of Foreign Exchange 外汇种类
17. Amount in Foreign Exchange 外汇金额
18. Balance by Currency 货币平衡
19. Authorized Bank or Dealer 指定银行或代理商
20. Signature and Seal 签字和盖章

Country	Currency	ISO	07/28/17	07/31/17	% Change	
ARGENTINA	Peso	ARS	17.79746	17.68950	-0.6066%	↓
AUSTRALIA	Dollar	AUD	1.254675	1.253663	-0.0807%	↓
AUSTRIA	Euro	EUR	0.852355	0.851158	-0.1404%	↓
BELGIUM	Euro	EUR	0.852355	0.851158	-0.1404%	↓
BRAZIL	Real	BRL	3.151397	3.134336	-0.5414%	↓
CANADA	Dollar	CAD	1.251108	1.248135	-0.2376%	↓
CHILE	Peso	CLP	650.9885	651.4836	+0.0776%	↑
CHINA	Yuan	CNY	6.741750	6.729877	-0.1761%	↓
CZECH REP.	Koruna	CZK	22.19862	22.18291	-0.0708%	↓
DENMARK	Krone	DKK	6.321448	6.312571	-0.1404%	↓
EUROPEAN UNION	Euro	EUR	0.852355	0.851158	-0.1404%	↓
FINLAND	Euro	EUR	0.852355	0.851158	-0.1404%	↓
FRANCE	Euro	EUR	0.852355	0.851158	-0.1404%	↓

Note: Currency Rates Per 1.00 US Dollar

Translation for the Tour Leader 领队翻译

1. Translate the following sentences into English with the words or phrases given.

(1) 大型百货商店大多不讲价，但经常用降价(slash price)促销来吸引顾客。

(2) 虽然逛夜市(night bazaar)你能讨价还价，但是记住这些市场购买的产品没有很好的保障。

(3) 为什么不让其他团员在直销店(outlet store)购买一些深海鱼油呢?

(4) 你必须到银行、机场或火车站的货币兑换处(money exchange counter)去兑换。

(5) 如果外汇兑换券(Foreign Exchange Certificates)用不完该怎么办?

 扫一扫，做翻译。

2. Translate the following sentences into Chinese with the words or phrases given.

(1) Hong Kong is the world's fourth largest exporter of jewelry (珠宝) and it has more jewelry shops per square kilometer than any other city in the world.

(2) This guitar is inexpensive (不贵), but it is still well made and easy to play.

(3) We will give you a written warranty (保证书) for the product you buy.

(4) When you make a purchase, it is always a good idea to find out the store's return and exchange policy (退货和退款规定).

(5) When you are leaving the European Union countries, please remember to take this refund form (退税表) with the item you bought to the Customs at the airport for stamping.

扫一扫，做翻译。

本章参考文献

[1] 王健民. 出境旅游领队实务[M]. 5版. 北京：旅游教育出版社，2016.

[2] 杨淑慧. 旅游英语[M]. 天津：天津科技翻译出版公司，2007.

[3] 曹景洲. 海外旅游领队业务[M]. 北京：中国旅游出版社，2011.

[4] 曹银玲. 出境领队实务[M]. 北京：旅游教育出版社，2012.

[5] 黄恢月，仉向明. 出境旅游领队工作案例解析[M]. 北京：旅游教育出版社，2008.

[6] 王远梅. 空乘英语[M]. 北京：国防工业出版社，2010.

[7] http://www.wendangwang.com/doc/4a5345890272ae788d74b1e3

[8] http://www.wikihow.com/Get-the-Best-Exchange-Rate-when-Traveling-in-a-Foreign-Country

Chapter 9

安全与应急处理
Security and Emergencies

Learning Focus 学习要点

- **Case Study**
  A Traffic Accident
- **Listening Comprehension**
  Accidents and Injuries
- **Situational Dialogue**
  Task 9-1 Tourist Missing and Items Lost
      —Air Tickets Lost
  Task 9-2 Illness and Care
      —Food Poisoning
  Task 9-3 Accidents and Injuries
      —Anklebone Fracture
- **ABC about Destination Countries**
  ABC about Switzerland
- **Consolidation**
  Practical Writing: Fire Warning
  Translation for Tour Leader

- ◆ 案例分析
  交通事故
- ◆ 听力训练
  事故与伤害
- ◆ 情景对话
  ①游客走失及遗失物品
  ——遗失机票
  ②疾病与护理
  ——食物中毒
  ③事故与伤害
  ——踝关节骨折
- ◆ 目的地国家概况
  瑞士概况
- ◆ 巩固练习
  应用文写作：火警通告
  领队翻译

Part One Case Study
第一部分：案例分析

A Traffic Accident 交通事故

In June of 2012, Mr. Diao paid 6300 RMB for a five-day tour to Singapore, Malaysia and Thailand. The tour was conducted by Shanghai JinJian Travel Co. Ltd,. On June 10th, 2012, Mr. Diao was knocked over by a motorbike when he traveled in Malaysia. His camera fell down to the ground, and his clothes damaged. Back in China, he entrusted the travel service to file a claim, but received only 3872 RMB from the insurance company.

Mr. Diao disagreed, he started the legal proceedings against the travel service in the Shanghai Luwan District Court, and requested the defendant to pay him 500,000 RMB for his economic and mental damage. The court entrusted a judicial appraisal center to have a medicolegal identification. The result of the report confirmed: fracture of the left lateral tibial plateau; and his left knee joint cannot move freely, which has reached the tenth class of disability. The medical expenses were far more than the amount that the insurance company was liable for.

After a cautious trial, the court finally issued an order: Taking into account the plaintiff's mental sufferings, the defendants should pay the mental damage. Then, the court judicially sentenced that Shanghai Jinjian Travel Co. Ltd should pay the plaintiff 340,000 RMB, including medical care fees, transportation fees, nutritional expenses, care services, camera repair fee, disability and mental damage solatium.

 扫一扫，看译文。

1. Discussions: How can you handle the case if you were a tour leader?
_____
_____
_____

2. Try to put forward more suggestions to the tour leader who is handling the case of traffic accident.
(1)_____
(2)_____
(3)_____

Chapter 9
安全与应急处理
Security and Emergencies

 扫一扫，有答案。

小知识

领队境外应急处理

1. 交通事故

(1)领队应该迅速抢救伤员。同时应沉着冷静，迅速将游客撤到安全的地方。

(2)领队应该对伤员进行止血及伤口包扎，尽快将重伤者送往就近医院抢救。

(3)如有重大伤亡，应立即联系救护车；保护好现场，以便相关部门调查处理。

2. 火灾

(1)游客应该立刻报火警。

(2)领队应该告诉游客发生火灾，并且带他们通过安全紧急出口到达安全的地方。

(3)警告游客不能乘坐电梯。由于火灾可能造成停电，游客会被困在电梯里。

3. 突发心脏病

(1)领队不能拿出自己的药给病人服用，因为他没有处方权。如果其他游客不是医生，领队也不能从他们那里取药给病人服用。

(2)领队应当让病人平躺在地，将他的头稍稍抬起。如果病人有减轻心脏病症状的药物，领队可帮助病人服下。

(3)领队应当立即拨打电话叫救护车，将病人送往附近的医院救治。

Part Two Listening Comprehension
第二部分：听力训练

Words and Expressions

account for		(在数量、比例上)占	rafting	n.	漂流
gliding	n.	滑翔，滑行	hazard	n.	危险
pedestrian	n.	行人，路人	signal	n.	信号

Accidents and Injuries 事故与伤害

1. Listen to the dialogue and fill in the blanks with the missing information you've heard.

 扫一扫，听一听。

117

Accidents and injuries account for a significant number of health problems for travellers (1) _____. Up to a third of all reported medical cases are due to avoidable accidents.

Accidents commonly occur on the roads, when (2) _____ and during sporting activities such as skiing, climbing, rafting, cycling, etc. Some tourists may, as more (3) _____ forms of tourism become popular, expose themselves to risks (surfing, water-skiing, winter sports, hang-gliding, etc.) which make them particularly (4) _____ should a disaster occur.

In many countries, road accidents are responsible for more deaths amongst tourists than any other (5) _____. When crossing the road, remember that the traffic may come from the opposite direction to the one in your (6) _____ country. Likewise, drivers in many countries do not observe (7) _____ crossings or traffic signals. Exercise additional caution when crossing roads while in (8) _____ surroundings.

扫一扫，有答案。

2. Fill in the blanks with the words and expressions given below and change their forms when necessary.

occur	cautious	observation	swim
avoid	dead	significance	direct

(1) Accidents and injuries account for a _____ number of health problems for travellers abroad.
(2) Up to a third of all reported medical cases are due to _____ accidents.
(3) Accidents commonly occur on the roads, when _____ and during sporting activities.
(4) The more active forms of tourism make tourists particularly vulnerable should a disaster _____.
(5) In many countries, road accidents are responsible for more _____ amongst tourists than any other hazard.
(6) The traffic may come from the opposite _____ to the one in your home country.
(7) Drivers in many countries do not _____ pedestrian crossings or traffic signals.
(8) Tourists must exercise additional _____ when crossing roads while in unfamiliar surroundings.

 扫一扫，有答案。

Chapter 9
安全与应急处理
Security and Emergencies

Part Three Situational Dialogue
第三部分：情景对话

Words and Expressions

| vomit | v. | 呕吐 | ejection | n. | 喷出 |
| toxicity | n. | 毒性 | preliminary | adj. | 初步的 |

Task 9-1 Tourist Missing and Items Lost 游客走失及遗失物品

Air Tickets Lost 遗失机票

1. Listen to the dialogue and fill in the blanks with the missing words or phrases you've heard.

  扫一扫，听一听。

(T=Tour Leader; L=Local Guide)

T: Oh, my goodness! (1) _____

L: What's the matter, Mr. Lin? May I help you?

T: Yes, Jack. Miss Luo's air ticket is lost. She told me she had (2)_____.

L: Has she checked her wallet or anywhere else?

T: Yes, she's looked everywhere (3) _____.

L: Has she been to anywhere with it this morning?

T: Let me see. Oh, yes. She may have left it in the shop (4) _____.

L: Where did she go shopping?

T: At the Smith's Jewelry (5) _____.

L: Don't worry. We still have enough time. I'll go there to see whether (6) _____
_____.

T: Thank you.

L: Don't mention it.

  扫一扫，有答案。

119

2. Listen to the dialogue again, and make a situational dialogue with your partner.

Task 9-2 Illness and Care 疾病与护理

Food Poisoning 食物中毒

1. Listen to the dialogue and answer the following questions.

 扫一扫，听一听。

(1) What's wrong with the tourists?

(2) How did they deal with the problem first?

(3) How were the tourists sent to the hospital?

(4) What is the relationship between the two speakers?

 扫一扫，有答案。

2. Listen to the dialogue again, and act it out with your deskmate. Pay attention to your body language.

Task 9-3 Accidents and Injuries 事故与伤害

Anklebone Fracture 踝关节骨折

1. Listen to the dialogue and rearrange the following sentences with the right order according to the sequence of the event.

 扫一扫，听一听。

(1) The doctor gave the tour leader a preliminary treatment.
(2) The tour leader's ankle was fractured.

(3) The tour leader went back to the hotel for a rest.
(4) The local guide called an ambulance.
(5) The local guide took tourists around the city according to the travel schedule.
(6) The local guide told the tour leader not to move and tried to comfort him.

 扫一扫，有答案。

2. Role play: Suppose you are a tour leader and your classmate is the local guide who has his leg broken. Make a situational dialogue.

Part Four ABC about Destination Countries
第四部分：目的地国家概况

Switzerland 瑞士

Switzerland is a landlocked country (内陆国) in Central Europe. It has borders with France to the west, Italy to the south, Austria and Liechtenstein (列支敦士登) to the east and Germany to the north. It is known for its mountains (Alps in south, Jura in northwest) but it also has a central plateau of rolling hills, plains, and large lakes. The highest point is Dufourspitze (杜富尔峰) at 4,634m while Lake Maggiore (马焦雷湖) is only 195m above sea level. The climate is temperate, but varies with altitude. Switzerland has cold, cloudy, rainy/snowy winters and cool to warm, cloudy, humid summers with occasional showers.

Switzerland's independence and neutrality have long been honoured by the major European powers and Switzerland was not involved in either of the two World Wars. The political and economic integration of Europe over the past half century, as well as Switzerland's role in many UN and international organizations has strengthened Switzerland's ties with its neighbours. However, the country did not officially become a UN member until 2002. Switzerland remains active in many UN and international organizations, but retains a strong commitment to neutrality (中立).

Switzerland is a peaceful, prosperous (繁荣的), and stable modern market economy with low unemployment, a highly skilled labour force, and a per capita GDP larger than that of the big Western European economies. The Swiss in recent years have brought their economic practices largely into conformity with the EU's to enhance their international competitiveness (竞争力). Switzerland remains a safe haven for investors, because it has maintained a degree of bank secrecy and has kept up the franc's long-term external value.

Switzerland showcases three of Europe's most distinct (截然不同的) cultures. To the northeast is the clean and correct, 8-to-5-working, stiffer Swiss-German-speaking Switzerland; to the southwest you find the wine drinking and laissez-faire (放任的) style known from the French; in the southeast, south of the Alps, the sun warms cappuccino-sippers loitering (闲逛) in Italian-style piazzas; and in the centre: classic Swiss alphonse and mountain landscapes. Binding it all together is a distinct Swiss mentality. Switzerland can be a glorious whirlwind trip whether you've packed your hiking boots, snowboard, or just a good book and a pair of sunglasses.

Read the passage aloud and choose the best answer to complete each statement.

1. The Switzerland has a central plateau of rolling hills, plains, and large lakes except for _____.
   A. glaciers   B. rivers
   C. deserts   D. plateau

2. Based on the text, which of the followings is NOT the neighbour of Switzerland? _____.
   A. France   B. Liechtenstein
   C. Germany   D. Australia

3. The climate of Switzerland varies with altitude, and has cold, cloudy, rainy/snowy _____.
   A. springs   B. summers
   C. winters   D. autumns

4. A distinct Swiss mentality comes from the binding of European cultures which are represented by _____.
   A. French, German and Italian cultures   B. English, French and Italian cultures
   C. French, German and Polish cultures   D. French, Dutch and Italian cultures

 扫一扫，有答案。

Watch the short video twice, and complete the following requirements.

Step 1: Watch the video and take notes of what you have watched or heard. Compare the notes with your desk mate.

Step 2: Watch the video again and fill in the blanks in the following sentences with what you have watched or heard.

Chapter 9
安全与应急处理
Security and Emergencies

Summary:

1. Numerous lakes also add to the picture-postcard look of this country. From banks to _____ alpine meadows, Switzerland has it all.

2. As it is home to the international Olympic Committee, Lausanne is also the _____ to some of the world's best ski slopes.

3. Environmental travelers will enjoy the fact that Geneva is a green city with 20 percent of its land devoted to parks, earning the _____ of park city.

4. Zurich will appeal to travelers with an interest in culture since it boasts more than 50 museums and over 100 art _____.

5. Lucerne is most famous for its fourteenth century Chapel Bridge, which is said to be the most _____ monument in Switzerland.

 扫一扫,看视频。

Part Five Consolidation
第五部分:巩固练习

Practical Writing 应用文写作

Fire Warning 火警通告

A fire warning is a warning issued by civil authorities to inform the public of major, uncontrolled fires (usually wildfires) threatening populated areas and/or major roadways. A red flag warning, a warning issued when low relative humidity and high winds and temperatures are expected, will generally precede any fire activity by at least one to two days. A fire warning will generally include information on the location and movement of the fire, evacuation instructions, and shelter locations. Read the following fire warning and tell tourists to take precautions.

Suppose you are the tour leader, orally translate the passage to the tour members and evacuate them according to the instruction of Fire Warning.

Outline:

1. Name and Address of the department 部门名称及其地址
2. Time/Day/Date 时间/星期/日期
3. Fire Threatening Location 火灾发生区域

4. Fire Threatening Address 火灾具体地址
5. Solution 应采取的措施

BULLETIN-EAS ACTIVATION REQUESTED
FIRE WARNING…CORRECTED
AMERILLO/POTTER/RANDALL OFFICE OF EMERGENCY MANAGEMENT
RELAYED BY NATIONAL WEATHER SERVICE AMARILLO TX
456 PM CST SUN FEB 27 2011

THE FOLLOWING MESSAGE IS TRANSMITTED AT THE REQUEST OF THE AMARILLO…POTTER AND RANDALL OFFICE OF EMERGENCY MANAGEMENT.

SEVERAL WILDFIRES ARE THREATENING THE FOLLOWING LOCATIONS: RICHLAND ACRES AND RANCH ACRES…AND THEN ALSO FOR TIMBERCREEK CANYON…PALISADES…TANGLE AIRE…AND LAKE TANGLEWOOD. IT IS RECOMMENDED THAT TOURISTS EVACUATE THE RIVER FALLS AREA OF RANDALL COUNTY. TOURISTS SHOULD EVACUATE IMMEDIATELY.

TOURISTS EVACUATING THE WILDFIRES IN THE WILLOW CREEK AREA SHOULD REPORT TO THE RECEIVING POINT AT THE PLEASANT VALLEY METHODIST CHURCH AT 316 VALLEY. THE RECEIVING POINT FOR THOSE TOURISTS EVACUATING FROM THE SOUTH WILDFIRES IS THE COWBOY CHURCH AT WASHINGTON STREET AND LOOP 335…HOLLYWOOD ROAD.

Translation for the Tour Leader 领队翻译

1. Translate the following sentences into English with the words or phrases given.

(1) 我会告知旅行社。他们会给您一个满意的补偿(a satisfactory compensation)的。

(2) 或许您可以去失物招领处(Lost and Found Counter)看看。说不定有人捡了交到那里去了。

(3) 领队在接待人数较多的旅游团时，最头疼的事就是客人掉队走失(get lost)。因此，要在出发前(setting off)做好防范工作。

(4) 在所有上报的就医案例(reported medical cases)里，有三分之一以上均由不可避免的事故(unavoidable accidents)造成。
(5) 无论发生任何事，只要领队冷静并高效(efficiently)处理，一切都会有满意的解决办法(solve)。

 扫一扫，做翻译。

2. Translate the following sentences into Chinese with the words or phrases given.

(1) The tour leader should make an effort to keep the injured tourist's spirit up (振作起来), as sometimes dealing with the emotional effect is much more important than the physical treatment.

(2) Have you made a photocopy (复印件) of your passport in case of emergency?

(3) The outbound tour leader should inform all members of not mentioning their personal (个人的) information to others.

(4) A breach of security (治安事故) means that the tourist has suffered: theft, robbery, fraud (诈骗), murder (谋杀) and their life or property has been endangered on the trip.

(5) In many countries, road accidents are responsible for more deaths amongst tourists than any other hazard (危害).

 扫一扫，做翻译。

本章参考文献

[1]陆建平. 现代旅游英语教程[M]. 北京：商务印书馆，2008.
[2]曹银玲. 出境领队实务[M]. 北京：旅游教育出版社，2012.
[3]王健民. 出境旅游领队实务[M]. 5版. 北京：旅游教育出版社，2016.
[4]黄恢月，仇向明. 出境旅游领队工作案例解析[M]. 北京：旅游教育出版社，2008.
[5]袁智敏，仇向明. 领队英语[M]. 2版. 北京：旅游教育出版社，2008.
[6]李娌，王哲. 导游服务案例精选解析[M]. 北京：旅游教育出版社，2007.
[7] http://v.youku.com/v_show/id_XMjgyNjkzOTM5Ng==.html

Chapter 10

离境回国
Departure from Destination Countries

Learning Focus 学习要点

- **Case Study**
  Dollars in Underpants
- **Listening Comprehension**
  Sending off the Tour Group
- **Situational Dialogue**
  Task 10-1 Preparations Before Departure
  　　　　—Wake-up Call
  Task 10-2 Check-out Hotel
  　　　　—Reservation for Shuttle Bus
  Task 10-3 Airport Check-out
  　　　　—Getting Aboard
  Task 10-4 Tax Refund
  　　　　—Inquiring about Tax Refund
- **ABC about Destination Countries**
  ABC about Kenya
- **Consolidation**
  Practical Writing: Tax Refund Form
  Translation for Tour Leader

- **案例分析**
  内裤里的美金
- **听力训练**
  离站送客
- **情景对话**
  ①离境前的准备工作
  　——叫早电话
  ②离店结账
  　——预订去机场的巴士
  ③办理机场离境手续
  　——登机回国
  ④退税
  　——询问退税
- **目的地国家概况**
  肯尼亚概况
- **巩固练习**
  应用文写作：退税单
  领队翻译

Part One Case Study
第一部分：案例分析

Dollars in Underpants 内裤里的美金

  Although the tour leader repeatedly reminded tourists to take with them all their personal belongings, some of them still left something behind in the hotel rooms. One day, after the trip in Alaska, they were prepared for checking out. Before getting on the bus, the tour leader reminded them of taking all their luggage. When everybody was seated on the bus, he asked again if they had left something in the hotel. No one responded, then, the local guide instructed the driver to set off.

  However, as the bus pulled out for only a few minutes, a tourist suddenly shouted: "Oh, I left something in the hotel!" The tour leader asked him what had been left. "It was the money, the dollars", he said. The tour leader instructed the driver to drive back right away. Luckily enough, the guy found his money.

  Why did this guy still leave his dollars in the hotel? It happened that the guy hid the dollar notes in the pockets of his underpants. As he was lazy, and didn't bother to wash it, he threw it into the waste basket carelessly.

 扫一扫，看译文。

1. Study the case carefully. Decide whether the following statements are true or false and write T for true and F for false.

(1) _____ The tour leader should remind tourists of taking their personal belongings with them before they check out the hotel.

(2) _____ The tour leader should help check the tourists' personal belongings in the hotel room before they set out.

(3) _____ The local guide cannot instruct the driver to set out without permission of the tour leader.

(4) _____ The tour leader should instruct the driver to head for the airport instead of coming back to the hotel.

(5) _____ In case that they failed to catch the plane, both the tour leader and the tourist should be held responsible for it.

Chapter 10

离境回国
Departure from Destination Countries

 扫一扫，有答案。

2. Divide the class into several groups for a brief discussion. How would you handle the case if you were a tour leader?

(1) _____
(2) _____
(3) _____

 扫一扫，有答案。

 小知识

离境回国时领队的工作

1. 办理乘机手续

帮助游客托运行李，换领登机卡。购买离境机场税，一般由境外接待社支付，多数情况下机场税包含在机票内。

2. 办理离境手续

将护照、机票发给游客。帮助游客填写出境卡，引导游客排队办理离境手续，有序通过移民局离境。

3. 办理海关手续

不同国家（地区）的海关有不同的途径限制，领队应充分了解离境国家（地区）的海关规定，协助游客办理通关手续。

4. 办理购物退税手续

欧美各大机场有购物退税专柜，登机前可凭购物凭证退税。领队应预留时间帮助游客办理购物退税手续。

5. 提醒游客登机

核实登机闸口并提醒游客注意，避免游客因购物而误机。

Part Two Listening Comprehension
第二部分：听力训练

Words and Expressions

dial	v.	拨打	digit	n.	数字
shuttle bus		班车	stewardess	n.	空姐
underneath	prep.	在……的下面	refund	n.	退款
custom	n.	海关	merchandise	n.	商品
spot-check	v.	抽查	credit card		信用卡

Sending off the Tour Group 离站送客

1. Listen carefully and identify mistakes in the passage. Underline the mistakes and fill in the right ones in the blanks.

 扫一扫，听一听。

The tour leader should confirm the time for the (1) _____ breakfast and the time for the delivery of luggage. Before they leave the hotel, the tour leader must remind tourists to (2) _____ pay cash if they take drinks and others in the mini fridges in their rooms. The tour leader must check the names, numbers of the tourists as well as the tickets and confirm the correct time and (3) _____ parking place for the tour group. He or she should reconfirm the seats, for the airline company may not reserve the seats if tourists who (4) _____ have Open tickets do not leave within 72 hours. If the tour group misses the airplane, the tour leader should contact (5) _____ the airline company to see if the earliest flight is available. The tour leader should try to catch it so that the tourists could come back according to (6) _____ the tour contract.

 扫一扫，有答案。

2. Listen to the passage again and answer the following questions.

(1) Who should arrange the morning call, the local guide or the tour leader?

(2) What else should the tour leader check besides the names, numbers of the tourists?

Chapter 10
离境回国
Departure from Destination Countries

(3) What should the tour leader do if the tourists miss the airplane?

 扫一扫，有答案。

Part Three Situational Dialogue
第三部分：情景对话

Words and Expressions

dial	v.	拨打	digit	n.	数字
shuttle bus		班车	stewardess	n.	空姐
underneath	prep.	在……的下面	refund	n.	退款
custom	n.	海关	merchandise	n.	商品
spot-check	v.	抽查	credit card		信用卡

Task 10-1 Preparations Before Departure 离境前的准备工作

Wake-up Call 叫早电话

1. Listen to the dialogue and write down the relevant information you've heard.

 扫一扫，听一听。

(1) The group is to take the early flight to _____.
(2) The tour leader wanted a morning call at _____.
(3) There are five rooms and the room number is_____.
(4) Each room has a _____ service.
(5) The computer will cancel the old time and_____.

 扫一扫，有答案。

2. Listen to the dialogue again, and act it out with your deskmate. Pay attention to your body language.

131

Task 10-2 Check-out Hotel 离店结账

Reservation for Shuttle Bus 预订去机场的巴士

1. Listen to the dialogue and write numbers in the blanks to show the correct order of the conversation.

 扫一扫，听一听。

(R=Receptionist; T=Tour Leader)

_____ (1) **R:** Could you tell me how many seats do you need?

_____ (2) **T:** I want to know if there is a shuttle bus to the airport.

_____ (3) **R:** Certainly, sir. May I know your room number?

_____ (4) **T:** We will leave early tomorrow morning. Could you help me make a reservation?

_____ (5) **R:** Yes, sir. We have a bus to the airport every other hour from 6:00 a.m. to 9:00 p.m.

_____ (6) **T:** 12 seats for the earliest bus.

_____ (7) **R:** May I help you?

_____ (8) **T:** Room 1218, Mr. Li.

_____ (9) **R:** You're welcome, sir.

_____ (10) **T:** That's right, thank you very much for your help.

_____ (11) **R:** Yes, Mr. Li, you reserved 12 seats for the earliest bus of tomorrow, is that right?

 扫一扫，有答案。

2. Listen to the dialogue again, and act it out with your partner.

Task 10-3 Airport Check-out 办理机场离境手续

Getting Aboard 登机回国

1. Listen to the dialogue and fill in the blanks with the missing words or phrases you've heard.

 扫一扫，听一听。

Chapter 10

离境回国
Departure from Destination Countries

(S= Stewardess; T=Tour Leader)

S: Good morning. (1) _____

T: Thank you, stewardess. Can you direct our group to our seats?

S: Certainly, may I see (2) _____?

T: Sure, here you are.

S: (3) _____

T: Thank you, miss. Where can we put our bags?

S: You can put the coat and small things on the rack (4) _____ and your bag here at your feet.

T: Can we put bags (5) _____?

S: I'm sorry. All carry-on luggage must be placed underneath the seat in front of you or in the overhead compartment.

T: Where is the button (6) _____?

S: Right here on the armrest.

T: Thank you.

S: You're welcome. (7) _____.

扫一扫，有答案。

2. Listen to the dialogue again, and make a situational dialogue with your partner.

Task 10-4 Tax Refund 退税

Inquiring about Tax Refund 询问退税

1. Listen carefully. Decide whether the following statements are true or false and write T for true and F for false.

扫一扫，听一听。

(1) _____ The salesgirl will write out a tax refund form for the tour leader only.

(2) _____ The Customs officer will check everything the tourists have bought.

(3) _____ The tourists can get the tax refund by showing the sales receipts.

(4) _____ The passport and refund form should be submitted for check except for the boarding pass.

133

(5) _____ Instead of cash, the tax refund can be transferred into the tourists' credit card accounts.

 扫一扫，有答案。

2. Listen to the dialogue again, and act it out with your partner.

Part Four ABC about Destination Countries
第四部分：目的地国家概况

Kenya 肯尼亚

Kenya is one of the world's most popular tourism destinations attracting millions of tourists over the past years. The country is endowed with attractive tourist sites, rich culture, striking geographical diversity and landscapes ranging from beautiful beaches, to animal parks and archaeological (考古的) sites. Kenya only has only two seasons: one rainy season and one dry season in a year.

The tourist destinations are well distributed all over the country. Currently, Kenya has six properties inscribed on the World Heritage List. These include cultural properties which are: Fort Jesus Mombasa (蒙巴萨耶稣堡), Lamu Old Town (拉穆老城), Sacred Mijikenda Kaya Forests (米吉肯达卡亚圣林) and Natural Properties which are Kenya Lake System in the Great Rift Valley (东非大裂谷), Lake Turkana National Parks (图尔卡纳湖国家公园) and Mount Kenya Natural Forest (肯尼亚山自然森林).

The Fort Jesus is one of the most outstanding historical sites and preservation of the 16th century. It was built and designed of Giovanni Battista Cairati with the aim of protecting the port of Mombasa (蒙巴萨岛) from external invasion. The fort occupies an area of 2.36 hectares.

Lamu Old Town is an exclusive tropical island and one of the oldest best preserved Swahili settlements in East Africa. It is one major center for the study of Islam and Swahili (斯瓦希里) cultures with many elite visiting for educational purposes. It is built in coral stone and mangrove timber. Lamu is also characterized by the simplicity of many structural forms enriched by ideal features such as elaborately carved wooden doors, verandas (阳台), and inner courtyards.

Sacred Mijikenda Kaya Forests (米吉肯达卡亚圣林) consist of 11 separate forest sites. It is yet another 16th century phenomenon with remains of several fortified villages locally known as Kayas. The land occupies 200km and is famed for bearing a living cultural tradition.

The boundless wilderness and big game of this Africa's region has long attracted adventure seekers from all over the world. No other African country can boast such an incredible range of landscapes, unique geographical features and species.

Read the passage aloud and choose the best answer to complete each statement.

1. The climate of Kenya is influenced by the diversity of its geography and featured by _____.

    A. dry in summer
    B. rainy in winter
    C. one rainy season and one dry season in a year
    D. hot in a year

2. Based on the text, which of the followings is NOT inscribed on the World Heritage List? _____

    A. Fort Jesus Mombasa
    B. Sacred Mijikenda Kaya Forest
    C. Yellowstone National Park
    D. Mount Kenya Natural Forest

3. _____ is one major center for the study of Islam and Swahili?

    A. Lamu Old Town
    B. Lake Turkana National Parks
    C. Kenya Lake System
    D. Great Rift Valley

4. What is the Kenyans' local language?

    A. English
    B. Swahili
    C. French
    D. Spanish

扫一扫，有答案。

Watch the short video twice, and complete the following requirements.

Step 1: Watch the video and take notes of what you have watched or heard. Compare the notes with your desk mate.

Step 2: Watch the video again and fill in the blanks in the following sentences with what you have watched or heard.

Summary:

1. Kenya is teeming with wildlife of all shapes and sizes, and it is the best place in the world to view _____.

2. The Mara is universally renowned for its exceptional populations of lions, leopards, cheetahs, elephants, _____, and giraffes.

3. You can watch the famous migration of _____ in Kenya that takes place every year from July to October.

4. And if you really want to get to places few others can reach, you can enjoy a truly amazing _____ service.

5. A classic African _____ is a travel experience like no other and there is nowhere better than Kenya.

 扫一扫，看视频。

Part Five Consolidation
第五部分：巩固练习

Practical Writing 应用文写作

Tax Refund Form 退税单

A tax refund or tax rebate is a refund on taxes when the tax liability is less than the taxes paid. Taxpayers can often get a tax refund on their income tax if the tax they owe is less than the sum of the total amount of the withholding taxes and estimated taxes that they paid, plus the refundable tax credits that they claim. (Tax refunds are money given back at the end of the financial year.)

If you filed a paper tax return, it could tax the IRS up to six weeks from that date it receives your paperwork to issue your tax return. If you want your tax refund more quickly, file your return electronically. The IRS typically issues tax refunds to electronic filers within three weeks.

Suppose you are the tourists, fill out the following registration form of tax refund. Don't hesitate to ask the tour leader if you have any problems when you fill in the form.

Outline:

1. Gender 性别
2. First name 名字
3. Middle name 中间名
4. Surname 姓
5. Date of birth 出生日期
6. Marital status 婚姻状况

7. City 居住地
8. Mobile phone 移动电话
9. E-mail 电子邮箱
10. Skype/ MSN 网络电话

Translation for the Tour Leader 领队翻译

1. Translate the following sentences into English with the words or phrases given.

(1) 到机场前，领队应确认出发当天旅游团准确的出发时间和地点 (place of the departure)。
(2) 领队应重新确认机位 (reconfirm the seats)，否则航空公司有可能不保留机位。
(3) 我只带了些个人用品及给朋友捎带的小礼物。我需要申报 (declare)吗?
(4) 登机时，请您出示登机牌 (boarding pass)。
(5) 如果游客错过航班，领队应争取让游客搭乘最近的航班(latest flight)离境。

 扫一扫，做翻译。

2. Translate the following sentences into Chinese with the words or phrases given.

(1) We are going to airport early tomorrow morning; I'd like to request a morning call(叫早服务).
(2) The tour leader should return their identity cards(身份证) or passports when the tourists arrive at the airport.
(3) The total amount of your payment and the refund amount(退税金额)will be clearly showed

in the form.

(4) Please go through the red channel(红色通道) if you have something to declare.

(5) You have three cartons of cigarettes and two bottles of wine. By the law, you must pay tax and fine (罚款).

 扫一扫，做翻译。

本章参考文献

[1] 曹景洲. 海外旅游领队业务[M]. 北京：中国旅游出版社，2011.

[2] 王健民. 出境旅游领队实务[M]. 5版. 北京：旅游教育出版社，2016.

[3] 袁智敏，仇向明. 领队英语[M]. 2版. 北京：旅游教育出版社，2008.

[4] 黄恢月，仇向明. 出境旅游领队工作案例解析[M]. 北京：旅游教育出版社，2008.

[5] http://usgovinfo.about.com/od/incometaxandtheirs/a/Getting-A-Tax-Refund-Quickly.htm

[6] http://www.tourism-review.cn/travel-tourism-magazine-kenyas-tourism-developing-fast-article1800

[7] www.wildfrontierstravel.com